THE MAN
IN THE
ROMAN STREET

Also by Harold Mattingly
CHRISTIANITY IN THE ROMAN EMPIRE

THE MAN
IN THE
ROMAN
STREET

by HAROLD MATTINGLY, F.B.A.

with an introducton by Alfred R. Bellinger
Lampson Professor of Latin, Emeritus,
Yale University

W · W · NORTON & COMPANY

New York · London

Library of Congress Catalog Card No. 66-11654
All Rights Reserved
Published simultaneously in Canada by
Penguin Books Canada Ltd,
2801 John Street, Markham, Ontario L3R 1B4.

W. W. Norton & Company, Inc., 500 Fifth Avenue, New York, N.Y. 10110
W. W. Norton & Company Ltd., 37 Great Russell Street, London WC1B 3NU

ISBN 0-393-00337-X

Printed in the United States of America

2 3 4 5 6 7 8 9 0

Contents

Introduction

ANCIENT HISTORIANS have given us works that are essentially
the records of great men and great events. The best of them
are works of art so fine that it would be stupid to wish that
they had been written in any other fashion. They are creations
of the heroic tradition, and their readers are expected to accept
the assumption that it is only the heroes—or the villains—
whose memory deserves to be perpetuated. Some of these
writers have been so successful in giving the color of their own
prejudices to the record of events that no amount of argument
to the contrary can do away with the effect of their brilliant
presentation. An admirable example is Tacitus, by whose
genius the characters of Tiberius and Nero are fixed in our
tradition, the historian's insight and his blindness both
immortalized. But modern readers, though it is hoped that
they will never be insensitive to the works of art, have a great
curiosity about the other half of the story. Persuaded that there
is a far higher proportion of people worthy of their understanding and remembering than antiquity would have allowed, they chafe at the exclusiveness of the Greek and Latin
authors and try by whatever means to bring to life the men
who were neither heroes nor villains but whose feelings and
actions were the necessary media of all acts of heroism and
villainy. Modern authors are apt to present the careers of their
great characters as a distillation of the lives of the characters'
contemporaries and to base their histories on the common
man. Now when subject and author are both modern the
writer has the advantage of an abundance of material from

which to select. But when the period is ancient, there is a serious dearth of information about the common man in the written record. The historians are not solely responsible; antiquity's indifference to the common man is apparent as early as the fountain of classical culture, the *Iliad,* where Achilles' Myrmidons are, indeed, very highly spoken of but do nothing at all. The war is strictly an affair of single champions. It is true that the *Odyssey* has a swineherd, but he is a "godlike" one, and in the final contest he is obviously to be classed among the heroes and not among the common men. So even the earliest of the historians had available almost nothing that would allow them to people the background of the mighty deeds they intended to relate.

But there is a class of evidence never used by the ancients and not always fully appreciated in modern times: the archaeological record, the remnants of actual human habitation and activity long buried in the ground. Besides the great foundations of the palaces and the magnificence of the treasures from the tombs, there are the ruins of humble houses, the simple votive offerings, the broken pitchers that are proof of the actuality of the common man. Among these a place of special importance is occupied by the coins, for there the economic and the aesthetic meet, the mere utility of the metal touched by man's fundamental instinct to ornament in a way that produces not only a pleasure to the eye but a message to influence the thoughtful user. The mint officials of the Republic, moved by family pride, pictured the great deeds of their ancestors and so kept alive the traditions of antiquity. Their successors in the uncertain days of civil war came to figure living people and so display their partisanship. In the early Empire, with which Mr. Mattingly is most concerned, the government had developed to a high degree the ability to use coin types as a medium of propaganda. At a time when most of the forms of publicity with which we are familiar had not yet been devised, the abundant coin types were used to influence men's minds far more than at present. They could explain and justify the imperial program; they could teach the virtues of loyalty and hold out the hope of prosperity and peace. It was the common man who was expected to be influenced, for, as Augustus fully realized, it was on the common man that the imperial power was based. Mr. Mattingly, from a lifelong familiarity with the written evidence and the archaeological, has produced this thoughtful picture of the common man, his beliefs and aspirations, his activities, his resources, and his limitations. The book is a good example of a class of work often demanded but seldom provided: a book written by a specialist, addressed to the general reader. It is a familiar complaint that the specialist will not write an intelligible general work on his subject and that the opportunity of reaching the great class of nonspecialists goes by default to the incompetent. The hesitation of the specialist is easy to understand. There is so little that is certain; hypothesis and deductions are so vulnerable unless they are supported by a mass of data; no matter how loudly the specialist insists that he is writing for the nonspecialist, his comrades in the field—the very people whose respect and approval he most desires—cannot be restrained from casting a critical eye on his imperfect work and he shudders at the prospect of the lethal comment "superficial!" But here and there a scholar from long meditation will have reached general conclusions that he has the generosity to share with students and those who have not had the opportunity to sift the evidence. To that honorable company Mr. Mattingly belongs.

For years he was in charge of the Roman coins in the British Museum and published the first four volumes of the *Catalogue of Roman Imperial Coins in the British Museum*, a truly colossal accomplishment that has given him an eminent position among the numismatists of the nineteenth and twentieth centuries. It is the kind of work that must be based on the patient confirmation of innumerable details, and it would not have been surprising if the technique of dealing with details had obtruded on the essays in *The Man in the Roman Street*, which are intended to give not data but conclusions. But there is no such obtrusion. Scholars in the field will recognize the traces of his earlier works and will remember the labor with which he assembled the structures here presented in their entirety. Students and those without expert knowledge, who want as complete a picture as possible of the Roman imperial scene, will find the interested and judicious reflections of a man who spent his life in acquiring a just and reasonable understanding of the period.

Alfred R. Bellinger

Washington, Connecticut
June 1965

Preface

WHETHER the study of history has a practical value may perhaps be doubted. In theory, of course, a study of past failures and successes should teach us what to avoid and what to pursue, and, in fact, it is hard to believe that some of the mistakes made in public life could be made by men who know their history well. But life is infinitely varied, and even if history does repeat itself it may only be with so much variation that each problem has to be thought out anew each time it recurs. More serious than this, it is seldom that the knowledge and the power to act on it come together in the same brain. Philosophers are seldom kings and dons even more seldom cabinet ministers. When a man with talent and interest for politics turns to history, it is too often only to find in it a setting for his own dreams. He takes what appeals to him and rejects the rest. One can see no reason to expect any good result from this method.

None the less, history has and will continue to have an absorbing interest. For, though it centers round politics and war, it goes beyond them to embrace the whole of human life. It is ideally the universal study. It is hard to imagine a subject that must not at times be studied from the historical angle, or a student who does not, at one time or another, yield to the attraction of history. As long as men are interested in life, they will be drawn by an overpowering curiosity to see how it has been lived in the past. They are still left with plenty of time to live in the present and even dream a little of the future.

History again is the mother of a great part of imaginative

fiction. The novelist, it is true, tries to interest us in individuals, their passions and their fortunes, while history puts in the foreground the fates of societies and nations. But what a wealth of individual experience is borne along on the tide of its mass movements! There is hardly a scene of tragedy or comedy in any but the wildest novel that cannot be paralleled somewhere or other in the recorded history of men.

History then should not be written only by experts for experts. Research has its proper place and function; the minutiae of research are proper food for the specialist; the truth of the historical picture will depend on his fidelity and skill. But, just as a line broken up into an infinite succession of points ceases to be a line, so history dissolved into an infinitude of details ceases to be history. The historian must dare to pass general judgments, to adopt definite attitudes toward life, to leave the ground of certainty and assurance and venture out to the disputable and uncertain. It is a necessary venture and a fine one. The old historians, who studied style, offered general views, and wrote to be read by the many, were more nearly right than those modern scholars who write only to be read—and with what difficulty?—by the few.

This is not to say that accuracy of detail is of no importance. It is only too readily surrendered by some who simply lack the natural capacity for it, by others who rank it below their prejudices and passions. Both forms of surrender are without justification. History is concerned not with what might possibly have happened, not with what you would like to have happened, but with what actually did occur. A statesman has been brought to trial and condemned, and your general judgment is that his condemnation was in the public interest. But, if it proves on investigation that the charges brought against him were false, you have no right to suppress the discovery. This should hardly need saying were it not that Clio, that lady of high honor, is expected by some to turn prostitute when required.

Facts, however, are not always accurately recorded, and our means of completing the record, by comparisons, analogies, or general considerations, are sadly inadequate. Besides facts, too, there are values. The old school histories that labeled the "good" and "bad" kings were not so absurd as they may appear. The value of life as lived under a bloody tyrant is likely to be below that of life as lived under an enlightened king, and it is as well at times to let the difference appear. It is possible to argue that moral standards are vague and variable, and, on that ground, to record events without passing any ethical judgment on them. But this is an excess of simplification, proper only to the specialist. It will give you the bare anatomy, the bones, the skeleton of history—but not the flesh, blood, and sinews, the play of the muscles, the flash of emotion on the face—all, in fact, that distinguishes the living from the dead.

Granted, however, the principle that history is to be recorded and judged by certain standards, there are grave dangers in applying it. The true standards by which to judge any period can only be learned by long and patient study of all its records, so that you may finally begin to think and feel as the men of the time thought and felt. To enforce the standards of your own time is obviously arbitrary and may be most unjust. Gibbon, in the *Decline and Fall of the Roman Empire,* is constantly to be found criticizing the later Romans because they were lacking in the humanism, the rationalism, the scepticism of his own age. Even Gibbon's genius cannot make this method other than absurd. The careful reader will soon discover that there are factors in Gibbon's theme, incorporated in his record but unaccounted for in his analysis, and, if he has the mental energy he will analyze them for himself. The temptation to interpret the past by the present will always exist. It may even be profitable occasionally to yield to it, if this is the only way in which we can realize that the past was as alive as we are today. But such interpretation involves a constant error: it ignores the "otherness" of past ages, while insisting on their likeness to our own.

Yet history, if it is to reach its true stature, seems to need some great general conception to illuminate it. Thus Thucyd-

ides felt profoundly the tragedy of the Athenian Empire and
saw in it a signal revelation of an underlying and recurrent
theme. Livy wrote nobly, if without full enlightenment, of the
growth of a Rome that might deserve to rule the world.
Polybius found in the "fortune" of that same Rome a key to
the history of the Mediterranean peoples. Recent years have
seen a number of histories, of very varying value, but all
illuminated by the same general idea—that of the analogy between a civilization and the individual human being. A civilization, like a man, can come into being, grow to maturity,
pass to senility, and finally die. History is the life story of such
superindividuals. A grandiose, perhaps even a magnificent
conception—within limits, a true and fruitful one. But it must
never be forgotten that the analogy is an analogy, and no
more, that it is at best imperfect, and that at points it breaks
down completely. A civilization is more than a succession of
customs and institutions, existing in material form: it is also a
system of thought, feeling, conduct, expressed in the successive
generations of individual men who share in it. It has in fact
both body and soul—but is there any true sense in which it is
an entity, as the individual man is seen to be? Again, even if
civilizations could be compared at all points to individuals,
they would not necessarily behave in the same way. As a matter of fact, there are episodes in the life of civilizations that
have no parallel in individual human life at all. A civilization
may break up into two or more parts, it may die in part and
survive in part, it may undergo changes unlike any that we
undergo. No, the comparison of state and man, macrocosm
and microcosm, must not be allowed too wide a domination.

One possible objection to history—that it is inevitably concerned with the past—will probably trouble us little today.
When the time scale of terrestrial evolution is applied, the
whole of recorded history shrinks to a span. So to the adult
mind that has once outgrown the absolute preoccupation with
the present that is characteristic of youth, all history is comparatively modern. The past begins with yesterday. The distance that we can retire into it without passing beyond re-

corded history is not very great; and real distance is not to be measured only by lapse of time. Just as a wireless station in England is in closer touch with and so, in a sense, nearer to a similar station in America than to a neighboring hamlet that does not yet know wireless, so we may today be closer to events in the history of Greece and Rome than to others that happened many centuries later, nearer our time, as we should usually say. To resent the study of the past if it seems to act only as a clog on the present and a brake on the movement to the future is reasonable enough. To reject it out of hand because it is "past" and therefore of no significance argues considerable confusion of thought.

It is quite certain, however, that very few men can spare the time to master even one period of history in its full detail. Either there may be abundance of material demanding long study or there may be the scarcity that seems to engender whole literatures over disputed shreds of evidence. What is needed, over and above all the requirements of the expert, is a series of carefully planned, carefully executed outlines of history, written by experts who have not lost touch with general interests and can thus mediate between the specialist and the wider circle of readers. Such outlines should receive as much attention and care as the most exact of scientific treatises. The fact that lines are to be drawn boldly and freely does not bring relaxation to the artist. A slight slip can still cause grave error.

These general considerations may perhaps seem to be rather loosely connected with one another and to lead to no particular goal. They have, however, risen in my mind out of a particular course of studies, and, to explain them further, it is time to turn to that. The Roman Empire has long been a problem to the historian. He can trace with some degree of accuracy how it came into being, but he is still pondering why it declined and fell. He has also to face the apparent impossibility of writing the history of a state whose history consisted less in political and military events than in the changing quality of the life it preserved in its cities. The layman has a vague idea of the Empire as something great and important that lies somewhere behind modern history, but he is much surer of its decline and fall than of its rise and prime. He will also know of it rather vaguely as the environment in which the Christian Church grew.

The study of the Empire is beset with grave difficulties. There is still no good general history, unless perhaps the *Cambridge Ancient History* may be held to fill the gap, and that fine work, from the very nature of its planning, lacks the unity of single authorship. The materials for study are most various and multitudinous. The literary tradition flows in two channels, pagan and Christian, which run long distinct courses and are seldom merged successfully in the thought of the modern scholar. But the Roman Empire is too interesting and too important to be consigned to oblivion. It marks a culminating point in history—the destinies of many peoples converging under the leadership of one, the establishment of stable government and world peace to a degree seldom realized on this imperfect earth, the decline of political liberty, the birth of a world religion. Whether for our comfort or our warning it indicates the sort of price that might be exacted from the individual for such protection and security as a state based on absolute authority can afford.

Obviously no one small book can go far towards supplying the missing interpretation of the Roman Empire to modern readers. But there is one aspect of the Empire, to which my work over many years has directed my attention, that is poorly represented in most of our histories but seems likely to attract and interest the layman. As I have worked out the details of the coinage of the Roman Empire and collated them with all that promised to throw light on them in literature and inscriptions, I have gradually realized that I was looking at something of quite extraordinary human interest—a mirror of the common man in Roman times, his concern, his hopes, his fears, his attitude toward his sovereign, his fellow countrymen, and his gods. What the exceptional man thinks and feels may be learned from his acts if he is a man of action; from his poems, his treatises, and his sculptures if he be poet, philosopher, or artist. The common man is lost in a background, usually quite vague and undefined. In one sense, this is as it should be, for it is the exceptional man who counts more than the mass. But, in another sense, it is the mass that is always right: "securus judicat orbis terrarum." In any case, even if it is the exceptional man that interests us, we have no chance of understanding him fully unless we can set him against his undistinguished fellows. A mountain cannot be seen as it is, without some sight of the surrounding plain.

What I have in mind is something like "A Short History of Public Opinion under the Roman Empire." It will derive something from the ancient historians, though the best of them were too unfriendly to the imperial system to be quite typical, more from the thousands and myriads of inscriptions set up all over the Empire and garnered in the great Berlin *Corpus* for us today. But it will rest even more on the series of Roman imperial coins, continuous from reign to reign and representing an uninterrupted appeal of the authorities to their public. The coins, if they do not directly represent, reflect public opinion, and, in the attempt to understand them, we are soon straining our eyes to see what the public opinion that they reflect really was.

Coins are essentially small objects, limited in their scope, laconic in their expression; to expect too much of them is to invite disappointment. But, whereas the *acta diurna* and the *acta senatus,* the imperial edicts, the rhetorical speeches that might have given us much fuller pictures of public opinion, survive if at all in fragmentary form, the record of the coins as regards the mass issues is virtually complete and acquires for that very reason a unique importance. And, further, the ancient coin—and, particularly, the Roman—had a wider function than the modern. Its types and legends were constantly changing and changing in sympathy with the movement of events. The coin was in fact steadily used as an instrument of publicity and propaganda. The man in the street certainly looked at it, studied it, and discussed it in a way that would surprise us. Even today, when we are dis-

tracted by so many other interests, if a government would
realize and revive this function of coinage we too might recover an interest in it.

Some may think that a study of a propaganda—the methods
of appeal to public opinion—should precede that of public
opinion itself. Actually the two studies are intimately connected and should be pursued together. I have chosen the
latter first, partly because propaganda is more obvious and has
been less inadequately studied, partly out of sheer personal
prejudice, because I am more interested in the masses of plain
people who are there to be cajoled and deceived than in the art
of cajoling and deceiving them.

The writing of this book involves several formidable difficulties that are wise to face bravely at the outset. The first is
the question of documentation. A book of this kind, if written
without constant reference to evidence, will be inaccurate or
worse; fully documented, it would be a burden to the scholar
and to the general reader an impossibility. As I am even more
anxious for the book to be alive than for it to be exact, I shall
ordinarily omit references to detail.

The second difficulty concerns the limits of time, which are
not set for us but must be, more or less arbitrarily, determined.
Since we must make a decision, we will begin with the accession of Augustus in 27 B.C. and continue down to the death
of Theodosius the Great in A.D. 395, taking in the Roman
Empire from its foundation to its final constitution as a Christian state. To break up the book into chapters, covering successive periods, would defect my main object; each chapter
would require its own subdivisions, and there would be no
room for larger general views to appear. The main arrange-
ment, then, will be by subjects. In a final chapter, I will try to
make good the deficiency by concentrating attention on the
factor of time and trying to make real and intelligible the
transit made in four centuries and more by that great human
creation that we call the Roman Empire.

A third difficulty, the most serious of all, remains—public
opinion in the Roman Empire. Very good, but where? At

Rome, in Italy, or in the provinces? The opinion of the upper or the lower classes, of the professional classes or the layman, of the townsman or the rustic? There is no complete answer to this difficulty. Ideally, a whole series of studies of different strata of public opinion would be necessary before we could sketch public opinion as a whole in a world of so many races, classes, and religions. Even if one were qualified to write such a series, one could not bring them to life in one small book. What encourages me to go on is the thought that I am only following in the steps of that succession of Roman civil servants who were responsible for the detailed ordering of the Roman coinage, who had to appeal to public opinion, and who had to make some decision as to the kind of public opinion they must appeal to. They contrived to maintain a certain unity throughout the coinage, despite inevitable breaks here and there: it does not dissolve into a series of disconnected appeals to different classes and orders. It is a unity of this kind that must be my aim. In theory, of course, the appeal was made to the vast mass of the citizens and subjects of the Empire, the innumerable clients of the emperor. In fact, the appeal was directed primarily to the masses of the people of Rome who shared in the emperor's largesses, applauded him in the circus or amphitheater, stood to cheer his advent to Rome, or crowded round his chariot as he drove in triumph to the Capitol. These were, so to say, the voters in the central and most privileged constituency of the Empire, the capital Rome herself—in civic status Romans, by race not only Romans or Italians even, but Gauls, Spaniards, Africans, Greeks, Syrians, and the rest, in culture slight sharers in the mixed Greco-Roman civilization of the age, in religion vague polytheists, believing more or less firmly in the old Olympian deities or in exciting importations from abroad such as Isis, Cybele, or Bellona. The newcomer from the provinces might at first feel out of place when thrown into the lump of the Roman poor. Very soon he would find so much familiar in their general view of life that he would lose his sense of separateness and, while adding his own spice of variety, lose himself in the mass. From time to time it will be possible to suggest what allowance should be made for divergence from our hypothetical norm.

But such divergence will not need so very often to be remarked, for the plan of my book is to cut below the surface of more or less arbitrary beliefs and reach those beliefs that lie deeper, held almost unconsciously and unconsciously shared even by those who might think themselves to be in irreconcilable conflict. Just as the Empire of many tribes and tongues settled down to use the two main languages, Latin and Greek, as its linguae francae and in each developed a common idiom, or Koine, easily understood from province to province, so, too, in thought one general frame built up on Greek and Roman models came to be generally used, like a universal language, throughout the Empire. There could never be general agreement about the arguments to be conducted in that language: there was something like agreement over the language in which the arguments were to be conducted.

On these lines, then, the adventure shall be essayed. If any period in the past of Europe deserves our study, it is that of the period that bridges the gap between the ancient and modern world. If it is always true that history should be even more concerned with life itself than with the accidents of experience, it is never more true than of the Roman Empire, which represented a society that had lived through a youth of restless instability into a middle age of settled calm.

The general lines of treatment once determined, it only remains to draw the ground plan of the work. There is no one plan forced on the writer by his subject matter; hardly any two writers would handle a single subject in the same way. It will be sufficient if the plan adopted is reasonably simple and easy to understand, is consistent with itself, and allows room for all the main themes of interest to be developed.

Here is a sketch of the plan that we shall follow.

The first chapter will take up and develop some ideas vital to our theme concerning the language in which public opinion can find expression. It will be suggested that there are forms of thought proper to different times and places that can hardly be escaped by men living in them. Unless we recognize these forms, we may read with complete grammatical accuracy the writers of a period without fully understanding their real meaning. These forms find expression not only in words but in pictures, as for instance in the types as opposed to the inscriptions of the coinage. This language of pictures must be studied and understood. In passing, we shall touch on some interesting questions about the function of symbolism in general.

The second chapter will set the stage on which the play is to be acted. It will sketch, in very brief outline, the character of the Empire, founded by Augustus, its organization and development down to Constantine and Theodosius, its central government, its system of defense, its component parts—nations, kingdoms, cultures, religious—its grades of society, its town and country life. It will give the material background upon which the studies of thought that follow are to be projected.

The third chapter comes to our main theme, the thought of the Empire, and treats first of religion, placed deliberately in the foreground, because it is here that the human mind seems to have found its main activity. It will sketch the traditional religions of Greece and Rome and their interplay, the old religions of the East and West—Anatolia, Syria, Egypt, Thrace, Africa, Gaul, Britain—and the "interpretatio Graeca" or "Romana" that came to be applied to them. Something must then be said of "syncretism," the blending of varied religious forms in one, of personal religion and the "mystery religions" of the Greeks, of astrology and magic. Finally we must mention some exceptions to the religious norms of the age—the Jews and Christians, with their protest against polytheism; the philosophers, more closely concerned with ethics than religion but sometimes willing to come to terms with popular religion and, later, forming a close defensive alliance with it against new attack, the agnostic and the atheist. Under all this diversity we may discover some forms of thought, common to all, and so fit to be incorporated in our common language.

Chapter IV will consider some distinctive features of this religion, polytheism, the many gods under one ruler: the relation to the chief god of his subordinates, the forms of worship, temple, image, sacrifice, and vow. The theory of "demons" and the role assigned to the gods as preservers of the visible world must also be considered.

Chapter V will deal with the belief in "virtues," or powers, existing either independently or in relation to a god or human individual. It will show how living and how tenacious of life this belief was and what light it throws on much in ancient thought that at first seems strange to us.

Without yet leaving religion entirely behind, we pass on in Chapter VI to consider its relation to the state and, in particular, the worship of the Roman emperor. The Roman had a very clear sense of a spiritual world underlying the material; it was natural that his state should always have its state religion. The worship of the emperor, restricted in extent as it was, did in part make good the absence of a general religion of the Empire. It must be considered in relation to Greek and Eastern practice and thought, to the philosophy of Euhemerus who regarded all gods as deified men, to the opposition from Jews and Christians, and to the persecutions that ensued.

The next chapter, Chapter VII, will ask what were the attitudes adopted by the all-powerful state to its subjects and by the subjects, on their side, to the state. How did the government attempt to justify or commend itself to the governed? How were its powers defined in terms of constitutional law, in religious belief, and in actual fact? What room if any was left for liberty?

One of the most vital issues in the life of a state is that of peace and war. How shall the government extend its sway or defend its rights, and what demands must it make on its subjects in so doing? Chapter VIII will discuss the particular forms in which this issue tended to rise under the Roman Empire.

If religion and politics are the main themes of universal

interest, there are others that attract large bodies of men and afford a valuable test of the quality of the civilization in which they live: such are literature, art, history, and science. Chapter IX will attempt to sketch the history of these under the Empire and to assess the degree of responsibility for their decline that should be attached to the government.

So far the emphasis has been almost entirely laid on public life. Chapter X will turn to the individual and give some account of his private life and thought, his personal morality, his family life, his interests and amusements.

Chapter XI will gather up under the heading "Present, Past, and Future" some general conceptions that are constantly recurring but cannot easily be imprisoned within any single definition. How did the Roman think of the past behind him, the future in front, and his immediate present between the two? The Golden Age, the Eternity of Rome, the "restoration of the times" will be some of the titles under which Roman thoughts on these lines will be explored.

A final chapter, Chapter XII, entitled "Transitus," will insist on that passage of time, that process of evolution, more or less ignored in the early chapters. Its main theme is the revolution of thought that finds its most obvious manifestation in the change from paganism to Christianity but which actually affected the whole of life. In conclusion, we may ask how far the Roman Empire may be held to have fulfilled its function in history, whether it is to be classed as a success or a failure.

THE MAN
IN THE
ROMAN STREET

I

Languages and Forms of Thought

In nothing more than in language are we the debtors to our environment and at the same time its slaves. Every child, in learning his native language, receives an immense contribution towards self-expression, but at the same time is led to express himself inside certain limits. As the child grows older, he learns the full use of the instrument and can affect to master it. But to the very end the habits of a language are so powerful as to dominate all but the strongest minds. There is a "genius" of a language who lays his spell on those who speak it. It has been well said that, when you learn a new language, you gain a new soul: the outward expression reacts on the inward life.

Examples can be found on every hand. Greek, with its rich vocabulary, its marvelous verbal forms, its particles, its genius for antithesis and balance, definitely encourages a certain restless vivacity of mind. Latin, with its weight and dignity, inclines toward solemnity and ritual. German, with its inversions and involutions, leads to real as well as quite unnecessary complexity. French, with its logic and limpid simplicity, invites the belief that, once correctly observed and stated, every problem is crystal clear. Language is the instrument created for a particular end—the expression of thought. Like every instrument, it has its limitations in use. The craftsman in expression really needs to have a number of languages in his toolbox and to select one or the other to suit each special need.

Somewhere behind these reflections hovers a problem, fascinating indeed but difficult. What is the mental experience immediately behind language? What is thought before it has found expression in words? Suppose two men of similar character and training but speaking different languages share the same experience: they will, of course, use different words to express the experience, but may the thought in their minds be the same? If there can be identity of mental experience for people of different tongues, then perfect translation from one language to another is possible. Actually, translation is seldom felt to be perfect. It would almost seem as if thought begins to be biased or deformed the moment it begins to find expression. The identity of mental experience that we might like to postulate is always eluding our grasp. In no language can free thought be expressed, for every language contains an element of determinism. A master of many languages might come near such freedom by letting his thought always find expression along the channel best suited to it.

To understand the thought of the Roman Empire we must know something of how it was expressed, of its language, in fact. The two main idioms, Latin and Greek, are well known, both in their vocabulary and their grammar. The scholar can read for himself; the layman can have recourse to reliable translations. But, by a convenient extension of use, we can mean by "language" much more than vocabulary and grammar. By extension language may include forms of thought that crystallize round certain words or phrases but are not fully expressed in them, when much more is suggested than actually said. It may include general ideas, associated with forms of words, but too big to be fully contained in them. And it may include pictorial language, the language of symbolism, comparable to written language but not capable of exact translation into it. From the laws of language, in this wider sense, even the genius cannot set himself free. Even if he protests against some of its conventions and strains to mould them to his own purposes, he can only make his criticism understood through the medium he is trying to criticize.

Language, in this wider sense, is the expression of the mental activity of an age. We are only imperfect masters of the language of our own time. What presumption, then, to expect to comprehend the language of another! Actually, our aim will be somewhat more modest. Just as a spoken language has only some hundreds of words in universal use among the gentle and simple while thousands and tens of thousands of words are reserved for the educated few, so the language of thought will have its first narrow, then its wider circle. It is only with the narrow circle of ideas that we shall mainly be concerned—ideas so obvious that they were used and exchanged by almost everyone without reflection.

Like is recognized by like. In studying an ancient civilization, you must begin by recognizing features sufficiently like what you know to be intelligible to you. It is the right and natural beginning. But, if you go forward honestly and intelligently from this beginning, you will soon meet surprises: where you expect like you will find otherness. If you seriously wish to enlarge your experience, treasure the surprises and shocks: they are the warning that you are crossing the boundary and entering on unknown territory. If the new experience now to be explored is genuinely there, it will soon be verified by test. It will be found to have its own consistency and its own laws: once acclimatized, you will come to breathe its air naturally. In reading ancient history, one should expect surprises: if you read long without them, you should pinch yourself to make sure that you are awake. The history of Greece and Rome is to us a strange blend of the like and the unlike, the known and the unknown, and that is what makes its study so exciting.

This imperfect resemblance between the classical age and our own may be felt even in studies that are purely linguistic. The Latin words *pietas, fides,* and *amor* are more or less equivalents of the English "piety," "faith," and "love," and may often be properly rendered by them. But search through the uses of these words in a big dictionary and you will go much further. It will appear that *pietas* to the Roman meant a special conception of "goodness" or "rightness" in various relations—to the gods, to one's family, to one's friends—for which English has no exact equivalent: that *fides* means not only faith, but also "trust," "loyalty," "confidence," "protection," including under one heading a number of ideas we tend to keep apart: that *amor* over part of the course follows the English love closely enough, but then parts company with it. Leaving single words and going on to groups of words or phrases, we find the little maxims, or words of proverbial wisdom, that pass from mouth to mouth, *gnothi seauton,* "know thyself," *meden agan,* "in nothing excess," *festina lente,* "hasten slowly." Here again we recognize ideas familiar to us, but in a setting not quite so familiar. On a lower level are the stock phrases of ordinary conversation, the clichés as we call them, expressions with more "form than soul," that do not so much express ideas as cloak the lack of them. Here, too, the same law of likeness and unlikeness applies.

Each age, then, has its own language, its choice words and phrases, its proverbs and its catchwords. But it has more than that. It has wide general ideas about life—about the gods, the state, the individual—which are not so much beliefs as ways of thinking or forms of thought, in which, by general consent, beliefs are expressed. A study of such forms of thought in the Roman Empire will fill our later chapters, but it will make our way clearer if we look at one or two in advance here. If you read in modern textbooks what is thought to be known about the religion of Rome, you will hear much of the building of temples, the introduction of new cults, the organization of priesthoods: you may easily miss the real content—the religious spirit that won for the Romans the title of the "most religious of nations." What needs to be added is a few general ideas, probably familiar to the scholars who write our books, but taken for granted and not expressly stated for the aid of the modern reader. The Roman felt life as dual: material and spiritual. There is a spirit, a genius, behind everything—behind man, behind the state, behind the natural world. This spiritual world is just the other side of things, not vague and ghostly, but the counterpart of the material. In this world dwell the gods and the expressions of their will; their *numina* (nods) are constantly coming through into our world. The gods are the guardians of the state and of the family. If they are offended, they show their wrath by special signs, "omens" or "prodigies," and it is essential, if you would escape ruin, to win their peace. You crave help by petitions and promises (*vota*), and you offer atonement by sacrifice, as you might with a human friend or foe. Roman religion was not unemotional, but it held emotion under strict control. Whether the stories told of the gods were to be taken seriously might be questioned: even in their attractive Greek form they were often silly or immoral. What mattered to the Roman was the close and continual concern of the gods for the things that he held dearest—his country and his home.

Did the Roman of the Empire believe in the many gods of polytheism? Even if belief in the literal truth of conventional stories may have begun to wane, the answer must still be "yes." A spiritual world behind the material and in touch with it and, in that world, many powers rather than one—these were still the prevailing forms of thought. When the Christians came into conflict with their pagan fellow citizens, they were still nearer agreement with them than either of them might be with a modern critic. The Christian did not necessarily deny the many gods of the heathen, but degraded them to the rank of daemons who usurp from foolish and frightened men the worship that belongs to the one supreme god alone.

Political thought under the Roman Empire was confined to a narrow frame of ideas, so universally accepted as almost to appear self-evident. Rome is the mistress of the world; her emperor is omnipotent and beneficent; peace, concord and liberty flourish within—but only within these limits. Discussions about aristocracy or democracy or representative government had ceased to be really relevant. Within this frame of ideas there was still room for debate—how far Rome should admit her subjects to her citizenship; what were the qualities of the perfect emperor; whether son should succeed father; how much liberty could still be left to the common man. Here

again the bitterest opponents would usually agree about the
form in which the problems were stated, whilst to a modern
observer it will often appear that nearly everything of real interest has been deliberately excluded from the debate.

The pictorial language, the symbolism, of the Empire is best
studied in the imperial coinage. Its pictures are derived from
ordinary life, from religion, from legend, and from history. A
temple, an arch, an altar may be shown literally for what it
was. Or some material object may appear as a symbol for an
idea that it inevitably suggests, as two hands clasped may
represent "concord." The great gods appear as objects of devotion and worship. But they may also suggest other meanings—
Jupiter may represent the emperor, his vice-regent on earth,
Juno the empress, or Hercules the emperor as the hero-
benefactor of the human race. The gods have their proper
attributes or emblems, and these can be used to represent
them. The thunderbolt will stand for Jupiter, the club for
Hercules, the caduceus—the serpent-wand—and purse for
Mercury. The world of minor deities, or virtues, has its own
law and order. Fortune can always be recognized by her
magic horn of plenty, her rudder, globe, and wheel, or Victory
by her wreath and palm. Scenes from legend or history could
also be used to suggest ideas. Aeneas escaping with his old father, Anchises, and his little son, Ascanius, from burning Troy
became a symbol of *pietas*. Brutus, the first consul, might be a
type of liberty, or Horatius Cocles swimming the Tiber a type
of valor. The language of pictures or symbols is less exact than
written language, but it is direct in its appraoch and can be
very powerful in its appeal.

It will be natural, in trying to understand what the citizens
of the Roman Empire felt, to begin with that body of thought
which they inherited from tradition and to treat it as if it were
something stable and unaltering. But it will appear now and
again, as we study the first centuries of the Christian era, that
what looks at first like the ripe old age of a system long past
its prime was at the same time the infancy of new ideas, destined to centuries of later growth and development. The

pagan tradition may be said to represent the one, the Christian the other—even if paganism was not quite uninterested in the future and Christianity had certainly not withdrawn all interest from the past.

II

The Roman Empire

To UNDERSTAND the spiritual and mental experience of the Roman Empire, it is necessary to know something of the material frame in which it was set. If there was more unity in that experience than at any previous period in history, this was not unconnected with the fact that material unity had been realized in a degree unknown before.

If you approach history with a doubt in your mind as to whether it has any general plan or purpose, you will find it difficult to retain after reading of the rise of Rome. There is something in the emergence of the Roman destiny, the Tyche or Fortuna, of Rome, that makes one feel, as one watches, that for once a corner of the veil is lifted and one is allowed to see something of the working of the powers that mould the world. In the *Aeneid* Virgil places the decision of the fate of Aeneas and his Trojans who are to found Rome in the council of the gods. In the pleadings of Venus for and Juno against the Trojans there may be a touch of pettiness, but in the final decision of Jupiter there is solemn dignity. "Imperium sine fine dedi!" ("I have given command without end!")

If we glance over the history of the ancient world in its broadest outline, we see first isolated areas—Babylonia, Assyria, Egypt—rising from the prehistoric level to cultures based on the use of metal and to the beginnings of historical life. The civilized area gradually spread. Persia follows Babylon and subjects the entire Near East, including Egypt, to herself. But one little world in the west, the world of Greece and her city-states, the Great King fails to conquer, and, for a century and a half, those cities develop life, political and intellectual, to a height as yet undreamed of. Greece finally succumbs, in her disunity, to the half-Greek Philip of Macedon, but his son, Alexander the Great, makes amends by leading the Greeks to their revenge, to triumph over the Great King and possess his Empire. Under the successors of Alexander, that Empire broke into pieces—political power resting mainly with Macedonia, Syria, and Egypt, while something of political freedom was still left to the Greek cities. Europe to the west and north was still lagging far behind in culture. Italy, however, was open to Greek influences, mainly coming through Etruria. From at least 700 B.C. Etruria built up a hegemony that lasted into the fifth century. When that collapsed, something like a dark age followed, as barbarous tribes broke from the center of Italy into the more civilized west and south. Out of the confusions of these years, one state, Rome, the city of the Tiber, rose to a supremacy over its neighbors that gradually extended to a political leadership of Italy. The one possible rival for the mastery of the western Mediterranean, the Phoenician Carthage, was checked, broken, and finally crushed in a series of wars. The more backward cultures of Gaul and Spain were gradually drawn into the wake of Rome.

To the Greek world, Rome was debtor for much of her culture and ideas. But when, after the defeat of Hannibal just before 200 B.C. she came into close political contact with the Greek powers, she soon began to show a superiority in statesmanship and military skill that was bound in the long run to carry her to the front. Drawn half against her will into these Eastern complications, Rome soon found herself able to assert herself against the kingdoms—Macedonian, Seleucid, and Egyptian. The issue begins to grow clearer. Rome was not only strong enough to meet any armed challenge, but she began to exercise a powerful attraction over the many who craved a stable government and a cessation of wasteful and purposeless wars. By invitation and by consent as much as by conquest, Rome found herself advancing to the role of arbitress for the whole civilized world. Then, when success seemed already so near, the Fortuna of Rome for a moment seemed to falter. The political foundations of Rome were shaken. Her supremacy in Italy was challenged by a revolt of her allies, maddened by the refusal of Roman citizenship. A series of murderous civil wars threatened Rome with the destruction that her foreign enemies had tried in vain to compass. At last, at a terrible cost, Rome won through. The democratic party triumphed in the person of Julius Caesar. From the fight for his succession, his adopted son, Octavian, came out the victor and, having beaten down all armed opposition, reconciled the mass of the survivors to the "new order," which he as "Augustus" introduced. Rome under a single ruler, a ruler who though only "chief citizen" at home was king or king of kings abroad, was ready to grasp the helm of world power, and, in fact, under Caesar and Augustus the edges of the Empire were rounded off. Up to the fringes of barbarism, to the Rhine and Danube, and to the African desert, the Roman legionary and the Roman tax collector advanced together. The last odd pieces were being fitted into place and the pattern made complete.

The new mistress of the world was a city-state, in origin not very unlike hundreds of others that dotted the countries of the Mediterranean. She had still the forms of government, under which she had grown from small to great—her senate, her consuls, her tribunes of the people, and the rest. But, to meet the problems of Empire, she had been compelled to accept the leadership of one man, and, detesting the name and appearance of tyranny and so unwilling to call him "king," she must create a new office, which, while respecting republican traditions, might carry the necessary powers. He must first of all be commander-in-chief of the armies. The old title of "imperator" by which the legions were accustomed to hail their victorious general was now reserved to describe this function; it has given us the modern "emperor." He could and frequently did hold the chief republican magistracy, the consulship, but he never incorporated it permanently among his powers. To retain his old connection with the democratic party, to appear as the protector of the Roman commons, and, at the same time, to be able to co-operate with the senate on many points of home administration, he accepted the tribunitian power, not as a yearly office but as one renewed year by year and virtually conferred for life. As imperator he would act in his capacity as single military chief; as holder of the tribunitian power he combined with the senate to represent the Roman state, "Senatus populusque Romanus." Though he was representative primarily of the junior partner, the *populus,* the initiative fell more and more to him. To these powers, either by addition or interpretation, were added others of a wide and varied kind—the direction of foreign policy, the management of the corn supply and of the police of Rome, a controlling voice in the elections of the chief magistrates. Above all, there was generally acknowledged in him an *auctoritas* surpassing by far that of any other Roman. Men looked to him as the natural person to take the initiative whenever there was any question about the proper person to act. The new consititution was a deliberate and judicious blend of old and new. In theory, the Roman *respublica,* or commonwealth, still subsisted; the senate and the magistrates continued in life. But, in fact, that chief citizen, the princeps, was bound to outweigh the rest. He was one against many; he had the power and the wealth to attach ever new clients to his cause, and, in case of serious crises, he held the decisive weapon, the army, in his hands.

The office of emperor, which was born rather of political necessity than of arbitrary human contrivance, was by the same necessity maintained and developed. The power of the emperor over politics, finance, and legislation steadily grew. His service gave increasing scope to energy and ambition of every kind. In a sense, there was no written constitution of the Empire, although it seems to have become customary to pass for each succeeding emperor a *lex de imperio,* which defined his powers. The actual course of Empire was largely determined by the growing mass of precedent, enshrined in the *acta* of the emperors. Unless an emperor ended in such disgrace that his memory was condemned, his *acta* continued to be valid after his death and normally binding on his successor.

There was one very grave weakness at the heart of the new system. The succession was never strictly regulated by law. The "constitutional" procedure, if one may use the term at all, was for the reigning emperor to select and present to the senate for acceptance the candidate whom he thought to be best fitted to succeed him. As it was customary on such occasions to conciliate the army and the people by a largess, the selected candidate might hope to succeed by the general consent. Where an emperor had sons of his body, he normally designated his successor from among them. Where he had none, he would adopt the man of his choice. This was as near as one could get to a satisfactory solution of a thorny problem. It gave Rome a marvelous succession of emperors—Nerva, Trajan, Hadrian, Antoninus Pius, and Marcus Aurelius. Natural succession had no similar triumphs to record. Commodus proved a sad sequel to Marcus, and Caracalla inherited the vices, without the virtues, of his father, Septimius Severus. At the worst, when an emperor fell by violence and the succession was disputed, it was the armies who decided: the praetorian guard or the legionaries of the provinces set up their candidate. In the third century of our era, amid the general confusions of the time, the succession was in constant dispute, the right of the senate to legitimize the emperor was almost lost, and the armies made and unmade emperors at will. Out of these distresses emerged the new order of the state as established by Diocletian and Constantine, with the emperor a king or despot in all but name, and the whole state—including the armies—prostrate before him. Diocletian attempted to establish succession by adoption in a highly elaborate form, but his system was too complicated for a world of scheming and ambitious men. After it collapsed, the old practice was resumed, except that the hereditary principle grew in honor and justified itself better in practice: it was certainly better suited to the absolute monarchy than the curious blend of opposites, represented in the early principle.

In the emperor Rome had her master, but she herself was mistress of the Empire. The Romans were the sovereign people, enjoying special rights and privileges. Roman citizenship was a prized possession, to which the most meritorious of her subjects might aspire. In the earlier days of the city-state it had been considered as an axiom that you held your citizenship in one city only. Rome broke away from the old rule and established her own citizenship, as a supercitizenship of the Empire that could be added over and above citizenship in one's original city. She had the wisdom to extend it, not ungenerously, to her subjects, and thus cut at the root what might have been a major cause of disaffection. Next to Rome came Italy, the partner in Empire, not the servant: that issue had been settled once and for all by the great Social War of 91–89 B.C. After Italy came the provinces, administrative districts corresponding more or less closely to the old kingdoms and groups of peoples of which the Empire was composed, from Gaul and Spain in the west to Asia and Syria in the east. These were governed by viceroys sent from Rome—originally consuls or praetors, later called proconsuls or propraetors when their office was extended beyond its original year in Rome. Augustus drew a clear and sensible line of distinction among them. The older, more settled provinces, where no large military forces were likely to be required, were left under the old magistrates, appointed by the senate. The newer provinces, which had still to be broken in to Roman discipline, were placed by the emperor under deputies (legates) with armies at their disposal. A few minor provinces were rather more directly controlled by the emperor and administered by his agents (procurators). Judea, in the time of Our Lord, with its procurator, Pontius Pilate, is the best known of these. Egypt, because of its geographic position and its wealth of harvests, received exceptional treatment. It was set apart by the emperor as his own domain, and governed by a special viceroy, the prefect of Egypt; the emperor himself was accepted as the successor of the pharoahs and Ptolemies. A few peoples, inside the general boundaries of the Empire but near unsettled frontiers, were allowed for a time to continue under client kings. Such were Herod the Great and his successors in Judea and its neighborhood. In virtue of the *majus imperium* that was credited to him the emperor could, in emergency, overrule even a senatorial governor. He could draw all the threads together in his hand. He was his own secretary for the colonies and dominions. Herein lay both the strength of the system and the weakness that denied it any brilliant development: such representation as the provinces had in their councils hardly went beyond matters of form and religion. There was not even the beginning of any plan for imperial federation. Rome and Italy, it is true, came in the fourth century to meet the provinces on the same level—but it was not that the provinces had risen, they themselves had declined.

Beyond the frontiers lay a single, civilized state, the Parthian Empire, and a series of barbarian peoples at various levels of backward culture. Only with Parthia was there question of what we should normally call "foreign policy"—the control of Armenia being the chief point in dispute. As far as the barbarians were concerned the one anxiety of Rome was to maintain the peace and security of her frontiers at the cheapest possible cost—partly by authority and moral suasion, occasionally by payment of subsidies, when necessary by force of arms. Extensions of the frontier were rarely undertaken, though one that occurred under the first Claudius has a special interest for English readers. He it was who revived an old project of Julius Caesar and made Britain a province.

The Empire had answered the world-wide craving for peace, and peace was and remained one of its main ends. But the army required to maintain that peace was certainly not large—perhaps barely half a million men, legionaries and allies included. An elite corps, the praetorian guard, the household troops of the emperor, were placed in Rome. The legions were disposed at strategical points along the most vulnerable frontiers—the Rhine, the Danube, the Euphrates, and the African desert. Allied troops completed the strength, while the older and more peaceful provinces could as a rule be safely left to local militia. The more favored service in guards and legions began by being restricted to Romans and Italians but was gradually extended to provincials as well. The allies were recruited largely from semibarbarous peoples, recently incorporated in the Empire, and were trained to local arms and methods of warfare. The right of the state to conscript soldiers was never surrendered and was occasionally, in emergency, exercised. But the service, although hard and long, had its own tradition and honor: there were still brilliant prizes for distinction, and there was a sound scheme of pensioning for the veteran. It was, therefore, easy as a rule to obtain the recruits required by voluntary enlistment. It was a paid, professional army that guarded the Empire, from Hadrian's Wall on the border to the forts of the Euphrates in the east.

Within the vast framework of the Empire there was room for endless gradations on a variety of scales. In political privilege, the Roman citizen stood out before all others. Next to him came the citizens of such cities of old fame as Athens, after them the citizens of the great mass of cities of the Empire, after them the country population living either without civic interests or only loosely attached to the cities whose soil they helped to cultivate. Between full Roman citizenship and the status of foreigner (*peregrinus*) stood an intermediate right, the *jus Latinum*—a right originally developed in Italy for the colonies that Rome planted to hold her territories and increase her manpower but now extended to the provinces and used as a kind of education for full citizenship. Within the body of Roman citizens, within each civic community of the Empire, ran the great divisions of political privilege or lack of it, of wealth and poverty. The guiding principle everywhere was the dominance of the few, marked out either by family distinction or by wealth. In Rome the higher nobility was represented by the senate—with the patricians as a select minority in their ranks—the lower nobility by the knights.

The senator was distinguished by the broad purple stripe on his toga, the knight by the narrow stripe. The emperor had a controlling influence on the composition of both bodies. He conferred the broad stripe on the senator-to-be, and assigned the public horse to those whom he judged fit to be knights. In the provinces, it was the senators of the cities (*curiae* or *decuriones*) who stood out above their fellow citizens. Under the early Empire the privileged classes were not without public spirit and paid a very fair price for the honors they enjoyed by contributing handsomely to the necessities or luxuries of their native cities. But, later, the burdens of rank came to exceed its advantages, and there was something like a panic flight to escape from the *curiae*—and this although the distinction between "privileged" and "unprivileged" (*honestiores* and *humiliores*) was still maintained and even recognized as justification for different treatment before the law. Wealth without rank was, of course, not unknown—particularly amid the body of freedmen who were often men of great practical ability and were not held back by any nice scruples from the more "sordid" businesses. But the wealthy man, who did not incur the emperor's displeasure and have his money confiscated, would normally advance in due course to rank and position and would then invest largely in landed property, that most gentlemanly form of possession.

Beyond all these distinctions was yet one more—the distinction between slave and free; for slavery, though probably already on the decline, continued as an institution through the whole course of the Empire. Slavery was illiberal and economically wasteful. It may have been inhumanly cruel, but it had one great mitigation. The slave could be set free and advance not to mere local citizenship but to the great prize of Roman citizenship itself. There were restrictions to hinder the unlimited emancipation of slaves, and the free slave was at first in a special grade, a *libertus,* or freedman, still owing certain obligations to his former master. It is easy to point out the danger to the state from the influx of such a stream of new citizens at a low level: as Juvenal remarked, "the Orontes flowed into the

Tiber." But, without some such safety valve, slavery could hardly have been maintained at all.

Of nationality with its possibilities of division and strife, the Empire had enough and to spare. It almost looks as if nationality's active principle were only to be discovered now among the barbarians across the frontiers. Inside them, it seemed to have lost its particular virus. Within the Empire, the most vigorous and warlike nations had already spent their strength Italians, Spaniards, Gauls had submitted their future destinies to Roman control. In Africa, long submission to Carthage had prepared the natives for submission to Rome; the more recalcitrant of the Punic elements perished in the destruction of Carthage in 146 B.C. In the East, the habit of submission to kings had undermined the love of freedom, and growing intercommunication between countries was already developing a kind of international spirit, even before the Roman Empire. The famous cities of old Greece were politically powerless and, as such, very humble members of the great system in which they were merged. But the prestige of Greek culture was immense. Rome owed and acknowledged a vast debt to it, and the new culture of the Empire can only be described as Greco-Roman—basically Greek, though strongly influenced by the politically predominant partner. The last struggles of nationalism in the Balkans died out in the great Pannonian revolt under Augustus and in more protracted disorders in Thrace, which ended in its incorporation in the Empire as a province. It is safe to say that there was no acute race problem in the Empire at large. Men of different races met freely in the commercial and social life, and quarrels along this line of cleavage became increasingly rare. The great Aryan mystery was fortunately not yet revealed.

To this general rule there was one remarkable exception, the Jews. As there was nothing peculiar at first in the treatment extended to them by the Roman government, unless it were an unusual degree of toleration of Jewish religious scruples, the cause must have lain mainly with the Jews themselves. They had, in fact, their treasured religion and their law, their sense of aloofness, of special destiny and privilege, their great abilities and virtues, and their wonted faults of greed and ostentation. The Jews alone of all the peoples of the Empire could never settle down for long, whether under the rule of native princes or of Roman procurators and governors. There was continual friction with other peoples—notably with the Egyptians in Egypt—resentment of Roman rule, outbreaks of fanatical fury when religion was touched, banditry, and assassination. The end was complete tragedy. The first great revolt, A.D. 66–70, ended in the destruction of Jerusalem by Titus. Great revolts that flared up over the whole East in the last years of Trajan were repressed with merciless rigor, and finally, after the crushing of the second great revolt under Bar Cocheba, the "Son of a Star," the old Judaism was completely uprooted. Hadrian profaned the sacred city of Jerusalem by founding on its site his own Aelia Capitolina; the Jews ceased to be a people and the "Wandering Jew" entered on his pilgrimage.

The great movement towards political unification that culminated in the Roman Empire of Augustus had its counterpart in a spiritual movement towards unity that was afterwards seen to have reached its fulfillment when the gospel of Christ was preached to the gentiles. The parallel was seen quite early by Christian writers and soon became a commonplace of thought. But at the beginning of our era, it was still a secret. The need for some unification of thought and belief to balance the political unity was no doubt felt. But the statesman, if he thought of such matters at all, would tend to look to a state religion, concentrated on the person of the emperor. The devout pagan might dream of a reinterpretation of the myriad forms of polytheism that would finally harmonize all those partial worships of the heavenly powers in one great system. The philosopher might hope to find some mode of refined interpretation that would reduce a chaos of obscurity and confusion to a reasoned order. The Jew, whose history might have taught him to expect a special destiny for his people and a special function to perform in bringing the gentiles to the worship of the true God, failed to be awake in the hour of his visitation.

As the norm of public opinion under the Empire we have decided to take the average Roman citizen—domiciled in Rome, neither rich nor cultured, but, by his mere residence in the capital, alive to political movements, specially favored by the emperor, or even pampered and spoiled by corn-doles, largesses, and public shows—simply because in him more than in anyone else public opinion could find a vent. Looking back over our survey of the different grades of privilege, classes, and races of the Empire, we may just raise the question of what corresponding divergences from the norm might be expected from each of these.

Within the body of Roman citizens itself there would be no little variation. The old nobility would look with some reserve on the "new order" that had raised one family out of many to a pinnacle of power. They would regard with dislike and apprehension the great extension of Roman citizenship, and, while still sure of Roman destiny, would resent the passing of the old Rome into a new Rome of inferior stamp. The lower nobility, the knights, less deeply rooted in tradition and attracted to the new field opened to them in the imperial service, would look with more hope and interest to the future, and, in case of dispute, might often side with the lower orders rather than with the senate. The great mass of Roman citizens outside Rome—in Italy and the provinces—would share in the pride of their privileged status, but would be less immediately interested in the life of the capital and might look with some jealousy on the spoilt masses of Rome. Men of the "Latin right" would be mainly interested in the advance to full citizenship. The slave must of necessity look to enfranchisement as his supreme good. The freedman, while still half fettered by his own past, could enjoy in prospect the full privilege which he could see awaiting his children. The provincials —subjects but not citizens of the Empire—necessarily stood a little aloof from appeals addressed direct to Romans. Yet, from an early period in the Empire, one feels that the voice of the government was meant to be heard by the Empire as a whole. The blessings that it promised—peace, prosperity, security, won by victory and valor—could not be confined to any one privileged order. The longer the Roman Empire stood, the deeper grew the conviction that, essentially, all the subjects of the Empire were Romans; when Caracalla extended the citizenship over the whole Empire in A.D. 212, he was really only recognizing an almost accomplished fact. Everywhere, of course, the city dweller was politically more alert and alive than the countryman who fed his flocks and tilled his fields. It was in the cities that life was quickest and most versatile, in them that new radical movements ate into the old conservatism. A curious example is to be seen in the use of the word "pagan" (*paganus,* "villager") to denote the devotee of the old polytheism. Under Augustus, it was in the citizens of the towns that you must look for the typical representatives of Greek and Roman religion and culture. By the fifth century, the townsmen have become Christians. It is in the villages that the old "Greek" spirit lingers; the *pagani* crave to be left alone to worship the gods who have always blessed their labors. If we look at society, from top to bottom in its class gradations, we may venture to say that political interests predominated towards the top, religious interests towards the bottom. The imperial government had a message and an appeal for each.

The Roman Empire began as a system of provinces and dependencies, grouped rather loosely round a very active and powerful center. Rome was the brain and nerve center, the Empire only the body. But, in time, as we have seen, something happened that was hardly the intention of the founders of the Empire; the distinction between citizen and subject almost ceased to exist. Romans who had acquired Roman citizenship without losing all their own interests and culture could never find complete political representation; the rule of the emperor was the best substitute for it available. Spiritually the change was complete and decisive. The word "Roman" was still one to conjure with; the old legends, the old symbols could still be used, but the inner meaning of them has changed. The "rebirth of Rome" in the fourth century was symbolized by the she-wolf suckling the first founders, Romulus and Remus. This Rome had very little relation to the city of the Tiber and its good old ways (*prisci mores*). It suggested the hope of the revival of the past in its happier features—a world of many peoples and cultures that had agreed to call itself Roman. There was an acceptance by the Empire at large of the forms of the Roman and Greek tradition, only comparable to the appropriation by the Anglo-Saxon peoples of the sacred literature and traditions of the Jews.

III

The Religion of the Empire:
General Survey

To PLACE religion in the foreground of Roman belief and to
devote three whole chapters to it may seem to require an apol-
ogy. Was not the mob of Rome engrossed by material pleasures, "bread and circus races"? Was not the paganism of the
Empire equally debased in practice and bankrupt in creed?

To deny any truth to these charges would be futile. Gross
materialism, intellectual apathy, scepticism in religion—all are
evident enough. Juvenal, the Roman satirist, mocks the man
whose only sincere prayers are addressed to Laverna, the goddess of gain. As for belief in a spiritual world, it is forgotten in
the cradle;

> "that the spirits of the dead and the
> realms below the earth are a reality
> not even children believe, except
> those who have not had their first
> bath."

But even if many Romans lived and died like beasts, absorbed in material things, it is Roman thought that is our
present concern and Roman thought that we must study, in
spite of those to whom it meant little—be they many or few.
The reader who is only interested in the material aspects of
the Roman Empire must satisfy his interest from other books.

So much admitted, there is a great deal to be said on the other side. Roman religion was quite shockingly practical. It was concerned essentially with things as they are and it did not venture after difficult and unaccustomed moralities. It implied a practical explanation of the world as we know it and practical precepts as to how to gain its prizes and escape its perils. It demanded from the plain man no great intellectual effort and no uncommon goodness. Even the laziest mind cannot simply experience life as a string of happenings, unexplained and unconnected. Roman religion offered an explanation, which had not yet been outlived or superseded, of life. Even the doubters still used the forms of thought it had provided.

If we look beyond Rome and Italy to the Empire as a whole, another consideration forces itself on our attention. Rome, we have seen, was early recognized as a state devoted in a peculiar degree to religion. But on the whole the peoples of the Near East had a deeper and more vital concern in religion than the rough barbarians of the north and west. The influence of these peoples was now directed, as never before, on Rome and was not directed in vain. Add to this the fact that the decline of political life left a vacuum in the mind that must somehow be filled, and that religion was the only interest, strong and widespread enough at the time to fill it, and you will understand how the early Empire may, not unjustly, be termed an age of faith.

This truth—for such it surely is—is mainly obscured by one defect of the Roman world. It had not, like later ages of faith, a single creed, universally accepted. There was no one religion general to the Empire. The cult of the deified emperors—of which more below—was to some extent an artificial creation and only partially fulfilled its purpose. The gods of Greece and Rome had been harmonized in one orderly system, to which the gods of peoples of other nations—Africans, Syrians, Anatolians, Egyptians, Pannonians, Gauls—might be loosely attached. The religion that was destined to win the Empire passed its infancy and youth in the shadows of obscurity, distrust, and persecution. Our general survey of paganism will reveal no single consistent theology but rather a set of general religious conceptions, accepted in varying interpretations by the many, a series of revolts from those conceptions led here and there by the few.

At the root of religious thought in the Empire lies the belief in many gods, or should we say rather in divine activities, or numina? In many cases groups of activities had been recognized and identified and could be assigned to particular persons—the major gods and goddesses—just as out of a set of activities you can realize the personality of a man. These major deities were fully recognized. Their form and character were familiar from myth and sacred history, elaborated in word or marble by poet and sculptor. The equations of Greek and Roman names had been settled, once and for all. Apart from these greater powers there was a plurality of minor ones, whose range was as varied as life itself—nymphs of sea, hill, and woodland, genii, or spirits, of persons and places, beneficent powers that find expression in social and personal life—Pax, Pietas, Concordia, and the rest—countless little powers, revealed at a flash in isolated acts and vanishing as soon as revealed. The world in fact was full of gods and their forms were many.

When fully realized, the gods were persons and, as the only real persons in our experience are human, they were therefore represented in human form. They had their own houses (temples) and images (idols) that attested their presence there. They demanded the customary dues of worship, the ritual words and acts, the prayer and the vow, the sacrifice, bloody or unbloody, and the garland, the procession. Just as devout service might earn prosperity and victory, so neglect might bring down divine wrath and, with it, disaster and defeat. That men may not be ignorant of what the gods will, there are signs provided for their guidance—signs given by the birds of the air (auspices), signs hidden in the entrails of beasts, and signs and wonders outside the natural order (prodigies, or animals that speak, monstrous births, statues in the temples sweating blood). The religious state, like the religious man, will pay most careful heed to these warnings that peace between gods and men has been disturbed. The sign, or prodigy, indicates the spiritual evil as clearly as the stain in a cloth betrays the drop of acid that has fallen on it.

Greece and Rome, we have seen, had brought their religious systems into concord—the Greek form, by its superior plasticity and beauty, always tending to prevail. But the problem of concordance was never ended; it was always coming up again for fresh solution. The underlying reality, it might be presumed, was unchanging, but who could tell the limit to its forms of expression, to the number of the gods and their activities? When you met the gods of another people, you might find one quite new to you, as the Thracian Dionysus was new at first to the Greeks; you might recognize one already familiar and simply note the difference of name; or you might find combined in one deity traits known to you in several and would have then to consider which of several names was most properly to be applied.

The Roman Empire was rich to excess in religious forms. There was Egypt with its Serapis and Isis and its animal gods, Syria with its many local Baals and its great Dea Syria, Atargatis, Anatolia with its Great Mother, Cybele, the war-goddess Mâ, and the moon-god Men. From the East came the Persian Mithras, the god of light. Apart from the greater deities there were countless local powers, with primitive idols and primitive rites, especially prominent in Anatolia, where the memory of old Hittite religion was not yet extinct. Africa had its Punic deities, already partly blended with native powers, while Spain, Gaul, Britain, and the Danube provinces still worshiped deities of a cruder character but with rites and ceremonies not quite unintelligible to the Roman.

The general principles adopted were toleration and interpretation. Toleration was easy. Worship of one god need mean no disrespect to another. There could not be one way only to so great a mystery; why feel surprise or indignation, if you find someone aiming at it by another path than yours? In

order that you might not only tolerate but understand one another interpretation must follow—an "interpretatio Graeca" or
"Latina," which noted the characteristics of the gods of the nations and assigned them their due Greek and Latin names.
The supreme god—usually the sky-god—would be Zeus or
Jupiter, the god of the sea Poseidon or Neptune, the city goddess Athena or Minerva, the earth-mother Demeter or Ceres.
Thus it came about that in most parts of the Empire the old
deities continued to be worshiped, but with Greek and Latin
names either superseding or reinforcing the original. Whether
the interpretation always went right through beyond the name
to the form and rite may well be doubted. Old tradition was
terribly strong. The gods and goddesses with Greek names
whom the early Christians encountered, let us say, in Asia
Minor, were often enough curious and hideous ancient idols,
having very little in common but the name with the radiant
presences of Olympus. A few major deities—Isis, Cybele,
Mithras—were too potent and too clearly characterized to be
subordinated to the old system. They maintained a position
apart, as special revelations of the divine given to special peoples. The same is true of such a religious curiosity as the animal worship of Egypt. Even there the Greek or Roman would
seldom be intolerant enough to deny that this strange worship
had some meaning for its devotees; he would be content to
leave it to them.

Had paganism not dispersed its energies over so wide a field
and had some genius arisen with the capacity to comprehend
the whole, some colossal system of theology might have been
deduced, some immense Pantheon erected in which every god
of every people could have found his appropriate niche. The
effort required to synthesize a world of religions would have
been immense, and there was no sense of its need urgent
enough to produce it. Where thought was most active in the
field of religion, it was in criticizing the old forms and preparing to exchange them for new rather than in rehandling them
for new uses. All that we find is a series of uncoördinated attempts to produce harmony among different types of poly-

theism, to which we usually give the name of "syncretism." Statues, for example, are found, showing one figure with the attributes of several gods—a suggestion that there is some higher reality of comprehending powers of which we only know part. Poets would sometimes note the identity of the Sun with Apollo of the Greeks and Romans, with the Egyptian Ra, or the Persian Mithras. The worship of Isis, the mother-goddess of Egypt, with its mystery and its gentleness, exercised a very powerful attraction. When she appears to Apuleius in vision in *The Golden Ass* she declares herself as the one divine reality behind all the goddesses whom the nations worship under a multiplicity of names.

Besides religion in its true sense lurked the ugly shapes of superstition and magic. The natural desire to know the future might lead to such dubious acts as necromancy. The natural wish to mold events to your will might lead you away from prayer to magic. Formulas of cursing, in particular, were thought to be very efficacious in revenging yourself on your enemies. Astrology, the art of tracing human destiny from the stars, had a very wide following often among the upper classes, who might hold themselves aloof from the forms of religion. Superstition, finally, grew like a weed in a variety of forms. The most pervasive of these, perhaps, was the belief in demons, petty spiritual powers that crossed and vexed human life at countless points. The theory of demons could be applied, as we shall see later, as an explanation of the whole system of paganism. Actually, the demons usually meet us as troublesome little powers without names, responsible for many private calamities, illness, and particularly for nervous and mental disorders—attributed to demoniacal possession. That many people had sufficient strength of mind to rise above these ignominious terrors is obvious. But the life of common folk was often darkened by this fear of evil spirits, just as the mind of the Middle Ages was haunted by the fear of death, and as sensitive souls down to our own memory have writhed under the dread of final reprobation and hell-fire.

Though Roman religion in its origins may have been

strongly rooted in the family, its balance seems by the time of the Empire to have shifted to the state. Domestic pieties might still exist, but on a plane below that of the great public acts of worship. An entirely new movement could now be observed towards a purely personal religion. Even the great deities, who formed the centers of national worship, were sometimes made the objects of personal devotion. In the Greek East a special type of religion, known to us vaguely as the "mystery religion," grew up, the essence of which lay in one's personal relationship to a god who promised help and consolation in this life and a blessed destiny hereafter.

The religion of the Empire was certainly democratic in a degree never known before. The upper classes—the nobler and better bred—despised or affected to despise the intimate personal devotions of the masses. They themselves were satisfied with the good things of the world; they could still find self-expression in public life; they could still set posthumous fame against the fear of death. How easy, from their point of vantage, to sneer at the "deeply ignoble desires" of the many that found expression in religion. The aristocratic contempt for the democratic view of religion has made a deep mark on human thought; it disguises itself under the most specious forms and appears in the most unexpected quarters. Yet here, if anywhere, the common man must be right. A god worth man's trust and worship must have some concern for him as man—not simply as a unit in a state, or as magistrate, consul, or praetor with the purple stripe.

Atheists in the modern sense were rare; *atheos* was used more as a term of abuse than a description. The name might be given by enemies to the Epicureans, who had their own peculiar idea of gods, or to the Christians, who denied the gods of the state. But in general the "fool" who "said there is no God" was hard to find. Irreligion, in the sense of absorption in present aims and a contempt for religious scruples, was, alas, all too common, but that is a matter that concerns the will rather than the mind. The agnosticism we have known as a kind of negative creed was itself rare, even if many, laymen as well as philosophers, preserved a discreet caution in accepting final explanations of the ultimate mystery.

The philosophies must be regarded apart. Their distinctive mark was that they were less concerned with religious orthodoxy than with the good life, that they were essentially systems of ethics, and that even truth and right thinking were prized more for their practical good than for their intrinsic excellence. The god of Plato or Aristotle was far removed from the notions of the vulgar. The fiery soul of the universe, taught by the Stoics, seemed to imply pantheism rather than theism. The blissful gods of Epicurus, the main condition of whose bliss is that they are not concerned with human life, might perhaps be the objects of private spiritual devotion. They were defiantly contrasted with the gods of the state, forever meddling in our affairs. But most philosophers were content to look tolerantly on popular religion; it might serve useful purposes, might be conducive to happiness and stability in the state. Their opposition, if aroused, found expression in politics rather than in religion; it was there that the martyrs of philosophy earned their crown. This was while paganism still flourished. When it showed signs of collapsing before its new rivals, the philosophers actually began to band themselves together in its defence. They had always been able to suggest possible allegorical or natural explanations of the grosser and absurder myths. Now they went further and began to discover reasonable justifications for the veneration of idols, the sacrifice of victims, and all the apparatus of pagan cult. From about the third century onwards, two schools of philosophy, usually known to us as Neoplatonism and Neopythagoreanism, acted in unofficial alliance with the old religious order, suggesting lines of explanation along which the old religious ideas might be harmonized with reason and good sense, and even providing the missing "theology" of paganism. It was not without some justification that the Christian zealot, the Emperor Justinian, closed the last schools of philosophy in Greece; they had come to be almost the last refuge in which the old paganism could find shelter.

The Jewish kingdom, with its stiff-necked pride in its traditions and its law, its abhorrence of idols, its strict adhesion to
the one true God, stood apart among the nations. It was often
the object of hatred and suspicion, yet by its very obstinacy it
won a certain degree of toleration. The Roman government
itself was tolerant, even beyond its custom, in dealing with the
Jews. That they should insist on worshiping one God alone
might be considered simply an idiosyncrasy of the race. But
the underlying conflicts were too deep to be solved by concilia-
tion. The Jews were dispersed, their sacred city profaned, and,
though they survived as a people, they ceased to be a state.

To the Roman government the Christians appeared first as
a mere sect of the Jews. They accepted the same sacred books,
and they claimed a Jew as their founder. Why they and the
Jews should always be at strife must have seemed a mystery. It
may have been the persecution of Nero that first revealed the
Christians to the world as a people apart. After the destruction
of the temple by Titus, the difference between Jew and Christian became apparent. In the final revolt of the Jews under Bar
Cocheba, the Christians were actually found to be in definite
opposition to him. Thenceforward, the Christians came to present a problem of increasing difficulty to the Roman government. They were certainly a peculiar people; they were certainly unpopular. They refused to worship the gods, insisting
on the supremacy of one God of their own; at the same time,
they paid extraordinary honor to their founder, who had
actually been crucified as a dangerous agitator by the Roman
governor of Judea. They were inclined to abstain from the
good things of life—from theaters, banquets, shows of amphitheater and circus. More than this, they were suspected of
horrible crimes—child murder, incest—and of a hatred of the
whole human race, suspicions that perhaps arose out of genuine misunderstanding of the Christian love feast and of the
prophecies of the approaching end of the world. Whenever
some particular trouble such as plague and famine vexed
Rome, its anger might veer towards the Christians, and the
cry would rise, "Christiani ad leones." The problem for the

Romans began as a plain matter of police. If the Christians were guilty of horrible crimes, they obviously deserved punishment. But even if they were innocent of them, they formed an association not licensed by government and were therefore liable to summary suppression, if, innocent or guilty, they disturbed the peace. As Christianity spread, however, it became necessary for the Roman government to adopt a general policy, and, even before Trajan, it was accepted as a principle that a Christian could be punished "for the name" if he persisted, when challenged. But danger from the Christians did not appear nearly important enough to suggest the complete suppression of them as a body, and to punish individuals for what was no crime in the ordinary use of the term was invidious and alien to the best tradition of the Empire. Provincial governors, therefore, received instructions neither to seek out the Christians nor to accept anonymous denunciations of them. When a Christian was brought to trial, his judge would usually exert himself to move him, whether by persuasion or force, rather than exact the extreme penalty. If the Christian could be induced to curse Christ and to perform a simple act of worship, such as offering a few grains of incense to the genius of the emperor, all was well; he had given satisfactory evidence of religious conformity and political loyalty at the same time. Under this system, the Christian Church grew and prospered, increasing mightily in numbers and beginning to draw to itself the wealthy and educated as well as the poor and simple.

But popular uneasiness grew. What was this new order, this "third people," that throve on misunderstanding and persecution and still continued to propagate its peculiar and dangerous ideas—its denial of the gods, its aversion to war and to military service, its extravagant reverence for virginity up to the point of abstinence from marriage? Bitterness was increased by the growing miseries of the age. As early as A.D. 249 the Emperor Trajan Decius adopted the extreme policy and attacked not the individual Christian but the Church as a whole. After a few years of persecution came an interval of toleration that was ended when Diocletian, under the influence of Galerius, strove once and for all to root out the whole Christian organization. The assault failed, and Constantine, succeeding to supreme power, recognized and regularized the triumph of Christianity. Through most of the fourth century, paganism lingered on, now on the defensive but still authorized and, to some extent, protected by the government. Julian the Apostate even tried to reverse the course of history and restore paganism to its old place. His plans died with him, and his successors, notably Theodosius the Great, became zealots for the new faith and, practically speaking, abolished paganism in all its outward manifestations.

When the conduct of the Roman government towards the Christians is studied as a whole, it is its patience rather than its cruelty or intolerance that strikes us; the worst abuses can nearly always be traced to local governors. But it is curious that men in authority were so slow to see how well adapted Christianity was, in many ways, to make good the obvious deficiencies of the old religion and to provide a single faith in which the Empire could be united. No doubt the real reason for this was that Christianity would not accept what was axiomatic to the Roman mind—the absolute supremacy of the state. It introduced a new rival loyalty and thus opened the way to conflicts that have not ceased to divide men and peoples down to our own day.

We have surveyed a wide field, taking in many points of view that only slowly, if at all, influenced the man in the Roman street. At the beginning he was certainly a polytheist. That was the form of religion in which he had been taught to think and act, and he had no tremendous urge to think religion out again for himself. Prayer and sacrifice were traditionally reputed to bring material blessings, and he would not take the risk of neglecting them. You might laugh at the gods, as you might in private at the emperor, but you were careful about showing any disrespect in public. Later, in the third century, our plain man became worried and lost much of his good nature. He became frightened about the future and was readily led to look for scapegoats. The gods were clearly angry, and how better appease them than by pursuing their enemies! But disaster followed disaster, and still the government seemed as unable to order the state as to crush the Christians. The strain and fear continued, and the plain man began to look for salvation from the new instead of the old religion. At some period—we cannot say exactly when—public opinion swung definitely in favor of Christianity; it was probably even before the persecution of Diocletian. The persecutors hoped to strike at the crucial moment, but they were actually too late. The general mood of the fourth century was tolerant, except insofar as the Christian Church began to persecute its own sectarians and nonconformists. By the time of Theodosius the Great the plain man was Christian, accepting the new religion more or less as he had accepted the old. The new ideals could not fail entirely to touch him; but he was still very much a pagan at heart—as indeed he still is today, in many cases.

IV

The Great Gods
and Their Worship

ABOVE ALL OTHERS stood the great gods of the Greek and
Roman Pantheon, the Olympians, acknowledged by general
consent to be twelve in number—Jupiter (Zeus), Juno
(Hera), Apollo, Diana (Artemis), Mercury (Hermes),
Neptune (Poseidon), Ceres (Demeter), Minerva (Athena
or Pallas), Mars (Ares), Venus (Aphrodite), Vesta
(Hestia), and Vulcan (Hephaestus). Closely attached to
this circle and not far behind it in importance came such gods
as Liber Bacchus (Dionysus), Hercules (Heracles), Castor
and Pollux (Castor and Polydeuces, or Dioscuri), and
Proserpine (Persephone or Kore). After them followed a
multitude of lesser deities, largely restricted to their local cults.
The personalities of the major deities were more or less closely
defined. Their sacred stories were familiar not only from the
archives of the temples but also from literature and art. Their
types had been standardized by great sculptors and were as
generally familiar as those of earthly potentates. Equally
familiar were their functions and their emblems or attributes.
Jupiter was the supreme god, god of the sky—in his Capitoline temple chief guardian of the Roman state. His attribute
was the thunderbolt. Juno was the queen of heaven, herself a
guardian of Rome and also a protector of women and of the
sanctities of marriage. She bore as distinguishing mark the

scepter of majesty. Apollo bore as emblem the laurel branch and lyre, with a tripod sometimes at his side. He had many functions—he was bard and prophet, archer, healer and destroyer, and charioteer of the sun. Diana, his sister, had for attributes the bow and arrow and the hunting dog. She was the queen of hunting and the wild, a goddess of war, goddess of the moon and (like Hecate) of the shades, and also a protector of women. To Neptune fell the rule of the sea; his appropriate emblems were the trident and the dolphin. Ceres was the goddess of harvests and the earth and also of the mysteries; her attributes were corn ears and torch. Mercury, god of gain and luck, patron of traders and thieves, carried the magic wand, the caduceus, and a purse. Minerva, guardian of cities and goddess of war but also patron of arts and crafts, bore, as a rule, the warlike emblems, spear and shield; at her side might be the Athenian owl—from the city to which the goddess had given her name. Mars, god of war, bore warlike emblems, shield and trophy. Venus, the queen of love and beauty, might bear the apple given to the most fair or might borrow warlike emblems from Mars, her lover. Vesta was the goddess of the hearth and its sacred fire. It has often been said, from ancient times to our own, that she was worshiped without an image. Whatever this may mean it was not strictly true, for her type on coins is as familiar as that of any of the other gods. She bears the scepter of majesty, the patera, or dish, of sacrifice, and the palladium, or sacred image of Troy, to mark her Trojan origin; Vesta and her fillets of power were among the holy things of Troy that Virgil's Hector entrusted to the safekeeping of Aeneas. Liber, the god of wine, bore wine cup and thyrsus and had a panther at his heels. Hercules, god of valor, servant of mankind, and slayer of monsters, bore as chief emblem his mighty club and carried on his arm the spoils of the Nemean lion. Castor and Pollux, the Heavenly Twins, knight and boxer, were friendly and kindly deities, saviors of men, especially kind to those in peril on the sea. They appear as horsemen carrying spears with stars above their heads in Phrygian caps.

The theoretical supremacy of Jupiter was never questioned but not always stressed. Throughout the *Aeneid,* Juno and Venus intrigue and quarrel, carrying their anger into the council of the gods itself. It is only in the final decision that the will of Jupiter, itself the law of destiny, must win. The other gods were far too clearly and fully realized to be easily deposed to the lower rank of virtues, powers, or angels of the supreme god. The working theory was that to each god was allotted a portion, a moira, within which he ruled, like a satrap or viceroy in a province; he was ultimately responsible to the supreme god, but there was normally no appeal from him. In the second and third century of our era, the need was felt to stress unity rather than diversity in the world of many gods. Jupiter was worshipped as *exsuperantissimus,* the "most high." Elaborate attempts were made to establish either Jupiter (with Hercules as his lieutenant) or the Sol Invictus (who could combine in one the characters of Greek and Roman Apollo, of Eastern sun-god, perhaps even of Persian Mithras) as acknowledged lord and master. But these were desperate attempts of paganism to escape the solution to which it ultimately came—the acceptance of the one God of the Christians. In its essence it was polytheistic; it worshiped the one and the many, with the stress on the many. It was always threatening to dissolve into a chaos of uncoördinated atoms and was only precariously held together by theories of the supreme god with his inner circle of peers grouped round him and, beyond them, wider and wider circles of powers, growing less and less defined to the point of complete loss of personality.

Under the Empire, the great gods had to extend their functions. From the beginning they had had various numina, or powers, and might at times be worshiped under names and with attributes not generally familiar. But now they had to represent for the provincial, as he became a Roman subject or citizen, the local deities of older days. Jupiter, Apollo, Minerva had cults attributed to them that would often appear strangely out of keeping with the original character of those deities. The pagan found less difficulty in this than we should; he realized the rich variety of the spiritual world and was not surprised to find it in different manifestations in different places. Something not quite dissimilar is still to be found in the worship of the Virgin Mary under different bynames in different places of southern Europe.

There were other powers, derived from abroad, that were too powerful in themselves to be completely assimilated. Cybele, the Magna Mater of Phrygia, might, it is true, be identified with Rhea, the mother of Jupiter; essentially, she continued to reign in her own right. Her idol, the black stone of Pessinus, was brought to Rome to give victory in the second Punic war. Later she was worshiped, crowned with towers, and represented holding branch and drum, with lions at her side. From Egypt came Serapis, supreme lord and sun-god, and Isis, the mother, the queen of the sea—Isis, the predominant partner, familiar from her sacred sistrum and often represented riding on the Sothis dog. Atargatis, the Dea Syria, had a wide following, whilst the Persian god of light, Mithras, first introduced to the West through Cilicia, was destined to win a remarkable popularity—especially in the army under the later Empire. The worship of the sun-god was very strong in Syria and neighboring lands and, as we have seen, for a moment came near conquering the Roman world. The image and cult of one local sun-god, Elagabal of Emesa, was actually brought to Rome in A.D. 218 with the accession of the emperor generally known as Elagabalus, who was a priest of this deity. The deity passed for a short while into the center of Roman worship. The official attitude towards all these foreign worships was definitely cautious. The beliefs were only very slowly admitted to full recognition. The plain Roman will have been less backward—either willing to accept foreign cults in the mass with the rest of religious beliefs and practices, or, perhaps, attracted himself by the picturesque ceremonies and emotional appeal that they offered.

It was from the lands of the old civilizations, from Asia Minor, Syria, the East, and Egypt that these great cults came.

From the other provinces it is hard to quote a single example of a local deity that reached what we might call imperial rank. It may be that Apollo Grannus, a healing god enjoying special fame in Gaul, found admission to the imperial coinage in the reign of Albinus; it is certain that a strange god of the mixed Punic and Libyan population of Africa did find a place in the coinage of both Albinus and Severus—natives themselves of Africa. As a general rule, the local gods kept within their own limited areas and did not penetrate to the center.

Of the forms of pagan worship, a good deal is known in general, in detail remarkably little. It is not often that anything like a full record can be found of the words pronounced and the acts performed in any of the major rites of worship. But, as it is the general forms that really interest us here, the lack of detail will not delay us.

The god needs his house to dwell in, his temple, so that he may be near and accessible to his worshipers—even if he is thought to have his true home elsewhere, in the sky, the sea, or the woodland. He will be represented by an image showing him in human form with his appropriate attributes. He might also be represented by some idol, some uncouth stock barely recognizable as human, or simply by some object such as stone, thunderbolt, or spear. If you had asked the expert—the priest—which form if any truly represented the god, you would have been inviting and would probably have got an evasive answer. The plain man would naturally think that the god was like the human representation of him. That, at least, was how he chose to appear to man and was at any rate the nearest one could get to his real being.

The worship of the gods was expressed in a variety of forms. There were prayers and litanies in which the solemn grandeur of the Roman language found its most perfect expression. There were gifts for the temples, sacred vessels and the like, and ornaments for the statues, wreaths for the head, necklaces, and bracelets. There might be processions or games in the god's honor. But most characteristic of pagan worship was the sacrifice, sometimes unbloody offerings of cakes or a few grains of incense dropped on the altar, but more often bloody, a bull, ram, pig, or goat struck with ax or knife and allowed to bleed to death before the god. The value of the sacrifice was, of course, supposed to depend on the grateful devotion of which it was a sign; even the victim, at a perfect sacrifice, was supposed to come willingly to the altar. But actually the whole system was hopelessly mixed up with commercial interests. As the gods conveniently preferred the parts of the victim most unfit for human consumption, great quantities of meat were left free for disposal and naturally found their way to the meat market. Here is explained at once the difficulty encountered by the early Christians about "meats offered to idols"; a large part of the supply came from the temples. Great vested interests grew up round this traffic in beasts for sacrifice, which fought, with the single-minded obstinacy of self-interest, against any reform that might seem to threaten them.

The sacrifices were normally offered in fulfilment of a prayer or vow (*votum*). The Roman was a serious person of a practical turn of mind, and he did not cease to be so in his religion. In asking the god to grant him something that he desired, he felt he must offer a "quid pro quo," as he would in supplicating a fellow-man. Thus the prayer will run "If thou wilt grant me to return safe home from my journey to Spain, then I will sacrifice to thee a ram"—or whatever it might be. Vows were made privately by individuals and publicly by states. In the Empire, the vows undertaken "pro salute Augusti" regularly at the beginning of each year and, with renewed emphasis, at longer intervals—five, ten, or twenty years—came to be an important feature of the religious life of the state. With the vows of the New Year were associated ideas, almost as old as time, about the renewal of all things and the coming of spiritual and material blessings through the person of the ruler. This businesslike character of the vow should not lead us to imagine that it excluded genuine religious emotion, still less that it implied lack of real belief. It is a matter on which feeling has certainly changed since Roman times. We tend to accuse the Roman of lack of spirituality; he would have retorted to us with a charge of "levitas." Even if he could have been made to understand that we were offering spiritual sacrifices to our God, he would still have insisted that there must be some material offering in token of them.

In the almost complete absence of any full record, we can only guess at the words and acts that accompanied the rites of pagan worship—not to speak of the music, which very commonly went with them. But it is reasonably certain that the rite was often dramatic in form; things done were as important as things said. The ritual of the Roman Catholic Church surely preserves more than a little of the essence of the ancient Roman worship. The very idea of a "sacrament," in the sense of a spiritual truth expressed by a material emblem, came very readily to a Roman. He was quick to identify or confuse the god with his gift—Bacchus with wine and Ceres with grain. This is often treated as if it were a mere trick of speech, but it is more than that. It is rooted in a deep habit of thought.

At this point, after our short survey of the great gods and their worship, it will be convenient to pause and answer one or two questions that force themselves on the attention. Was paganism still alive under the Empire or simply a moldering corpse? If it was still alive what did the thoughtful man make of it, and how did they criticize it? What did it mean to the plain man? And, finally, what, if anything, does it mean to us today?

The first question is easily answered. Paganism was certainly alive under Augustus and continued to live for centuries after him, actually showing some signs of revival at the very time when it was declining to its fall. The forms of pagan religion continued to be kept, the worship in the temples to be maintained. The occasional neglect of some special temple of Juno Sospita under the late Republic or of Divus Claudius under the Empire proves nothing to the contrary. The world of thought, in which the great gods of Olympus were the chief powers, or numina, in the universe, continued to be the only world in which most minds could move freely. Writers and poets continue to refer to the gods, with a greater or less degree of pious fervor. The mass of the people still used the old language and observed the old rites. The imperial coins, which speak continuously from the government to the citizen, use a vocabulary that is to a quite extraordinary degree religious. The statement so often made, that by the time of the Empire paganism was moribund, is simply untrue; it can only be supported by selecting part of the evidence and unduly weighting it, while completely ignoring the rest.

What *is* true is that paganism was already—had in fact been for centuries—showing defects that aroused uneasiness and invited criticism! The old stories of the gods were excellent material for poetry and art, but how could you accept them as literal truth? They were often both immoral and absurd. Perhaps, then, they were allegories, suggesting inner meanings— the grand movements of the natural order or illustrations of moral truths. The practices of religion too may seem crude. Can it be true that a god is really no more than a man in the grand scale, that he must have a temple to live in, that he can have any need of gross material offerings such as the blood of sacrifices? Here too the philosophical mind tends to look for inner spiritual meanings under the coarse exterior. From Epicurus and his followers came a new objection. All— statesmen and commoners—seemed at least to be agreed that, whatever the gods were, they were very actively engaged in human affairs, public and private; they were in fact "busybodies," polypragmons. How was this belief consistent with the dignity of the gods? How consistent with the felicity men agreed to predicate of them? Epicurus told of gods living in perfect peace in the spheres between his worlds (intermundia), unconcerned with mortal affairs but still able to impress and enrich the mind with something of their own calm. It tells us a great deal of ancient religion that Epicurus was commonly condemned as an atheist. The objection to paganism that comes most readily to a modern mind—the objection that the oneness of God is almost forgotten in a chaos of so many powers—began now to come home to the Roman.

He was coming into close contact with people like the Jews and Christians, both of whom maintained emphatically that God is one, not many. But in spite of all the force of this objection, the Roman was slow to yield to it, and, even when he finally accepted Christianity, he made no slight effort to harmonize it with pagan instincts, still uneradicated. If the gods of the nations were no true gods, what were they then? Mere nothings, the work of men's hands, silver and gold? In a sense, yes. But surely, in view of the activities that they aroused, something more. One explanation, very popular at times amongst the Christians, was that they were not gods but spirits, demons, intermediate between God and man, disobedient to God and hostile to man, and striving to secure from man, their terrified and deluded victim, the honors that properly belong to God alone. Finally there was the laughing skeptic, to whom all human life is a puzzle and a joke, and religion in particular, with its exaggerated promises, was a special butt of his mirth. Lucian of Samosata, who lived in the second century of our era, is an outstanding example of this class—supreme alike in his incredulity, his irreverence, and his wit. But such men are always exceptions; they have nothing to tell us that will either help us to live nobly or to die in peace. "How should he think of death in such a prime?" That is really all that Lucian, in the prime of his own intellectual faculties, has to say. All that finally remains are bare skeletons and grinning skulls of what once were men in a hopeless and lightless hell.

If paganism was not dead, what did it really mean to the plain man? Tradition partly? What had been said and done from time immemorial? Not a creed, for paganism never had or could have one, but an acceptance of, or at least an acquiescence in, certain explanations of how the world ran. Not a system of high morality (rather the reverse some might say) but a sanction for the traditional and primary duties— family affection and love of country. The plain man is no philosopher and does not care to worry his head about the remote and unknown; let the philosophers who raise the doubts and difficulties settle them themselves! But religion meant something. It was clearly not without the will of the gods that the Roman state stood firm and that Rome ruled the world. Though the great gods were no doubt more concerned with the state than with the individual, they did not forbid access of private citizens to them, and there were always the many minor deities who stood in more immediate relationship with plain human interests. Our plain man would no more give up all the practices of prayer and vow than he would abandon all the forms of thought underlying them; in each case there would have been left that vacuum which nature abhors.

If this were all, it might perhaps be said that paganism to the Roman of the Empire was not so much a religion as a substitute for one. One must walk warily when one tries to press beyond forms of belief and worship to the religious sense to which they minister; it is only too easy to leave the realm of fact and lose oneself in a haze of suppositions and guesses. But long study will, I believe, convince the honest inquirer, as it has convinced me, that our Roman had a deep and genuine religious sense, which we can partly come to understand, and that paganism was in harmony with that sense. There are two worlds, the material and the spiritual, but the contrast is not between something present and something remote, the world that is and the world that is to come, but between two aspects of actual life as we experience it. The spiritual world, like the material, is multiple, with ultimate unity behind its variety. There is close and continual correspondence between the two worlds, and religion is mainly concerned with a right observance of the duties that arise out of that correspondence. Spiritual causes produce direct results in the material world; the material object is made to be the outward and visible sign of an inward and invisible grace. The insistence of the Roman Catholic on the real presence in the sacrament is, it seems, pure Roman, and this is not, of course, to express any judgment on the doctrine itself. So, too, with the doctrine of the resurrection of the body—that too seems to be very Roman in meaning. The Roman pagan of the Empire had no settled belief in immortality, but, if he could once be convinced of it, he would readily go on to believe that the flesh rose with the spirit. Body and spirit are only known to us in union in one person and, if you really mean anything by resurrection and are not simply spinning words, then the two must rise together. Of the more personal side of religion, a little more will be said in a later chapter. Here we need only note that a craving existed for something more intimate than the chief public forms of paganism supplied and that it was not entirely frustrated; even the great gods, whose primary concern is with society and the state, were not infrequently made the objects of personal devotion. However much the statesman and philosopher might object, religion was steadily becoming more democratic.

To admit that the paganism of the Empire was a living force, with some real value for its adherents, is not to suggest that it was the truth—still less to wish for its return. The recrudescence of paganism in modern Europe, with its harvest of terrible evil, is a sufficient warning against such a folly. But, in a sense, paganism is always with us and perhaps always will be. It has a sort of common sense of its own, a certain recognition and acceptance of things as they are. The intellect is always incurably pagan; it distrusts the visionary and the ideal. If only for our own protection, we need to realize the force and vitality of paganism. What happens when a vital belief in the one God is absent is not necessarily a pleasant and tolerant deism or even an easygoing natural life without religion. Man may come under the compelling influence of spiritual forces of inferior quality that, particularly when acting through groups, strongly suggest the working of evil spirits. It is unfashionable nowadays to personalize such forces. We have largely given up the old forms of thought and substituted for them forms borrowed from science; we think of forces like electricity rather than of persons like ourselves. The reality, no doubt, is only imperfectly held by either form, old or new. But the early Christians, who came up against the hostility of the pagan gods, as well as the pagans who sued for their grace, were equally convinced that they were real—as real as anything imperfect or evil can be—and we gain little by rationalizing them away, unless we have realized the experience out of which they grow.

V

Minor Deities, Genii, Virtues

THE MAIN HALLS of the great Pantheon of paganism are still
more or less familiar to modern visitors—partly from memo-
ries of the classics, of the New Testament, and of early Christian writers, partly from the lasting impression made by the
great gods on literature and art. But there were in it a number
of side chapels, by no means unfrequented in antiquity but today hardly known except to a very few specialists. It is not
only their minor importance that has caused them to be forgotten; the language in which they are referred to is often not
easy for a modern reader to understand. But with a little study
it is still possible to recover it.

Polytheism admits of the greatest possible variety, not only
of many divine powers but of many orders of the divine. Of
the great gods we learned something in the last chapter; it is
now time to turn to some deities of subsidiary rank. In this
multifarious world that we experience the Roman saw countless revelations of divine activity—numina as he called them.
They might be referred to one or another of the great gods,
who thus revealed themselves in acts of will. The great gods
might even be called numina, or powers, though that was by a
transference of meaning. But there were many numina that
could not be so assigned. These were isolated expressions of
divine will, like that superhuman voice that sounded through
the streets of Rome to give warning that the Gauls were at
hand. It was a "voice and nothing more," but the Romans rec-

ognized in it a numen and even assigned to it the name of "Aius Locutius." Numina of this kind may be almost infinite in number; they are, as it were, the atoms, the small dust of the spiritual world. Every activity of country life, every act in trade or profession, every expression of personal life may be considered to be under the ward of its own little god. There is a god to teach you how to plough and how to harrow, a god to teach the infant how to suck and how to walk, and so on; there are gods of nurture and gods of marriage. Gods of this kind have sometimes been named *Sondergötter,* or "separate gods," because their being is entirely contained in the single activity over which they preside. The Roman was cautious and, in case of any doubt, wanted to be sure of invoking the appropriate deity. To please him—and perhaps to satisfy their own love of curious ritual—the priests worked out elaborate formulae of invocation, known to us as the *indigitamenta.* A rather simpler method was to invoke a number of these little gods under a group name; thus, under the Empire, dedications to the *di conjugales, di genitales, di nutritores* (gods of marriage, birth, and nurture) still occur on the imperial coins.

Next come such groups of minor deities as the penates, the gods of the domestic store, and the lares, who were perhaps at first deified ancestors but in later use were spirits closely connected with places—particularly the *lar familiaris,* the "spirit of the home." Other lares were the nymphs of mountain, wood, and stream, a sort of collective manifestation of the great Mother Earth. There is the large and important class of "genii," or spirits, of persons, places, and things. There is the "genius loci," the spirit of some particular site, the genius of the senate, of the army, or of the Roman people. Each individual has his genius, or *Juno,* as it is properly called for the women. This genius is, in a sense, the life of the race. He is invoked with particular reverence on the birthday, and presides over the *torus genialis,* the marriage-bed. He is, as it were, a guardian angel or protector during life and may be held in some sense to outlive the individual in whom he has been manifested. Statius, when he writes a consolation to the widow of Lucan, who still honors her famous husband after his death and has a bust of him in gold, speaks of such remembrance as being the "vitae genialis origo," source of the genius's life. The many little gods, who attend each stage of human life, may be regarded as so many different aspects of the one genius. Of the special reverence paid to the genius of the emperor we shall have to speak at some length in a later chapter.

Not unlike the genii are the *fortunae,* the special "fortunes" or "lucks" of people and places. Fortuna was indeed an independent goddess, universal in her sway, an object of very real worship under the Empire. The modern worshiper of success would have naturally paid his vows to her. But there were also many lesser fortunae—Fortuna Manens, Fortuna Huiusce Diei—the special fortuna of great men like Sulla or Caesar. "Remember that you carry the Fortuna of Caesar," said Caesar to the boatman who was frightened by the storm that overtook them as they tried to snatch a passage from the Epirot coast to Italy. Fortuna, in this sense, is very near to Genius; the genius of the emperor is hardly to be distinguished from his fortuna, or *tyche.* A special development of this idea of fortuna was in relation to cities, each of which might be held to have its own fortuna, its *tutela,* or tutelary spirit, its tyche. Notably famous was the Tyche of Antioch, represented as a woman, crowned with towers, seated above a flood, in which the river god Orontes is seen swimming. The Fortuna Populi Romani expresses in one way exactly what the goddess Roma does in another.

Of the demons something has already been said, and a very short recapitulation will suffice. The idea is Greek rather than Roman in origin, and its development is to be traced more in the provinces than in Rome itself. The demons are, in some respects, like the Roman numina, but they are conceived of more positively and personally. Intermediate between gods and men, they haunt the middle air and make their presence known by visitations, usually of a hostile character, such as disease or madness. The Christians saw in them a convincing explanation of the gods of the heathen—no gods, in truth, but restless and disobedient spirits, striving to usurp the worship owed by man to God alone.

Finally we come to the "virtues" or "powers," which played a large part in popular belief but are lightly treated and often misunderstood in modern books. At first glance, they look enough like the personifications with which we are still familiar—Justice, Virtue, Beauty, Truth. But, whereas the modern personification is a cold, vague figure, with no fixed attribute and little appeal to the imagination, distinguished more by its capital letter than by any more serious claim to personality, the ancient virtue was something far more alive. Virtue was a deity—usually a goddess, in harmony with the grammatical gender of the name—clearly realized as a person in human form, and in that respect like the great gods, with definite, recognizable attributes and with definite functions to fulfill. Virtue was capable both of receiving worship and of being invoked in prayer. What one sees here is, in fact, one more variation of the idiom of paganism and polytheism. Life may be divided into a number of departments, each presided over by a moral power. Where harmony is in question, Concordia is ready to be invoked. Where there is danger from famine, fire, or sword, to whom should we turn but to Salus, or Health, herself? To whom but to Felicitas for success in all our undertakings? Just as the world may be conceived of as an infinite series of numina (isolated manifestations of divinity) or as a system of genii (spiritual essences of material things) so, too, it may be seen as a set of provinces, each ruled by its presiding virtue. The general idea of virtues may perhaps seem to be less primitive than some of those that we have been discussing; in actual fact, it can be traced back to an early date in the Roman Republic. The virtues enjoyed a remarkable vogue under the Empire and continued in full vigor down to the very end of paganism. When Saint Augustine attacks such paganism as still survived about him among the Romans of his age, he devotes a considerable amount of attention to the cult of the virtues—clear evidence that it was still alive and active.

The natural preference of the normal man for the good explains why beneficent powers are selected for worship; as Cicero says, it is proper to "consecrate" (assign divine honors to) virtues, not vices. But there were occasional exceptions—a temple might be dedicated to Mefitis, goddess of plague, or an unscrupulous adventurer might set up altars to Effrontery and Shamelessness. Closely related to the virtues were the *res exoptandae,* objects of desire, such as Spes (Hope). But the distinction is much less in Latin than in English: to the Roman, the goddess and her gift were almost indistinguishable.

The "virtues" could stand alone as independent powers, naturally to be invoked whenever their special range of activity was touched. In every case it was wise to select the appropriate power—Felicitas when you wished for success; Salus when you were in special danger; Concordia when there was special need of peace and harmony in personal or other relations. But they could also be brought into relationship with other sets of ideas, and out of these blends of belief new ideas of some interest emerged.

The virtues could be related to the life of the individual man. As he learned to venerate the virtues, which could be expressed in his own action, he came to recognize that he, like the whole world, was "full of gods," and so to realize the immanence, as well as the transcendence of the divine. How much more readily could the application be made to the man of exceptional powers! To pay honor to those powers was a ready way of acknowledging his pre-eminence. The great individual emerged earlier in Greece than in Rome; it may well have been in the eastern provinces that the Roman governor first grew accustomed to seeing altars dedicated to his virtues. But, in any case, Rome was not slow to learn. Caesar, the dictator, dedicated a temple to his own *clementia,* the mercy that had schooled his heart to spare his political opponents. Under the Empire, the worship of imperial virtues was one of the most effective and common ways of paying honor to the emperors and bringing them very near the divine. It is of sufficient importance to require separate treatment in our next chapter.

The virtues might also be related to the great gods, whether as satellite powers or as functions, entirely subordinate to them. The very earliest Roman religion seems to have known such powers as Salacia (the "leaping" of Neptune) or Moles Martis (the "strivings of Mars"). Fides, Victoria, Virtus might be closely associated with Jupiter; Felicitas with Mercury, Salus with Aesculapius. In the last phase of paganism, when, in its death struggle with Christianity it strove to study and explain itself more clearly than ever before, the major deity would appear as a kind of solar system surrounded by a swarm of satellites, or one might even advance a step further and make all other deities and powers subordinate to one central, supreme god.

The Christian Church, finding the world of virtues present in current thought, was quick to apply it to its own uses. God is supreme and one, but He has His messengers or angels—seen in many aspects, but in one special aspect as His own attributes or virtues. The Angels of Victory and Mercy take the place of the pagan Victoria and Clementia. The Peace of God is an angel, armed at every point to repel the assaults of the evil one. In some of the lives of the martyrs, angelic powers, or virtues, are seen descending to the help of the suffering faithful. Jesus Christ himself could be interpreted as the supreme manifestation of the *virtus,* or power of God, including in himself all other powers. As one apologist writes, "He is God indeed," and "God of the inner powers." When Saint Ignatius was brought before the Emperor Trajan at Antioch, he was interrogated about the claim that he made to be a Christophoros, one who bore Christ in his own person. Trajan showed some curiosity about the meaning of this claim and asked the saint, "And do you not suppose that we carry in ourselves powers that give us valor and victory over our enemies?" Trajan was thinking here, not of Jupiter or Mars, but of Victoria Augusti and Virtus Augusti. He recognized some-

thing that he could understand in the claim of the saint, however presumptuous such a claim must have seemed to him
coming from someone so obscure. One is reminded of the
meeting of Oliver Cromwell and George Fox—great man of
action and great mystic. George Fox spoke of the "inner light"
and Cromwell, listening with deep interest, broke in to say
that he fully understood what he meant, but that the light of
which he spoke was a natural light, the light of reason.

Christianity in its triumph absorbed into itself not a little of
pagan thought, and by reinterpretation retained it for its own
use. Throughout the fourth century, when the pagan gods
were already banished from the coins, the virtues were still
allowed a place. This was not because they were pure abstrac-
tions like our modern personifications but because they belonged to a world of thought readily capable of interpretation
in a Christian as well as a pagan sense. Victory was worshiped by the Romans with special fervor as the power by
whose aid they had won and continued to hold their Empire.
Her altar stood in the Senate House, and even under the
Christian emperor incense was still offered on it; it seemed
ominous to remove it. But at last the pressure of Christian
opinion proved too strong, and the Emperor Gratian was induced to take the decisive step and remove the altar (A.D.
383). The pagan party in Rome rallied and a few years later
made an impassioned appeal to the Emperor Valentinian,
younger brother of Gratian, to restore the goddess. Sym-
machus, prefect of the city, was the mouthpiece of the pagans,
and very ably he pleaded his case. He begged for some reverence for the great traditions of the past, for some toleration in
the troubled world of the present. Rome herself might plead
that she had grown old in the old beliefs—let the debate as to
their truth or falsehood rest for a moment—and ask only to be
allowed to keep what was still left of them. The ultimate
truth—whatever the Christians may say—cannot be so simple
or so easy to find; it is impossible that there should be only
one road to lead to the supreme mystery. Saint Ambrose of
Milan met eloquence with eloquence and plea with plea. The

altar of Victory was not restored by Valentinian, nor, except for a very brief restoration by Stilicho, did it ever regain its old place. But the thought of Victory meant too much to the Romans to be banished with the altar. Right down into the Byzantine Empire the victorious power of the emperor remains perhaps his chief attribute, and the favorite acclamation is still "Auguste tu vincas!" Christian thought was equal to the occasion. As Saint Augustus expressed it, though you could not properly speak of Jupiter sending Victory to execute his pleasure, there was nothing to bar you from saying that God sent forth His angel to carry the triumph to that party that deserved his favor. Where the heathen goddess Victory had stood on the coins the Christian angel of Victory continued to stand, and, curiously enough, in the change from pagan to Christian she had not changed her form. She was still winged and still bore the victor's wreath and palm. This is perhaps the only case in which the transition from pagan goddess to Christian angel is absolutely clear, but there are certainly others to be found for the looking. The last two of Milton's angelic orders, "Thrones, Dominations, Princedoms, Virtues, Powers," clearly derive from the goddesses which we have been discussing. Just one other figure may be mentioned who survives in medieval art and story, the lady with the rudder, globe, and wheel, with gifts that she bestows at her caprice. She is none other than the pagan goddess Fortuna, now relegated to a curious half-existence between fable and reality.

The ancient virtues were distinguished from modern personifications by their superior vitality and by the firmness of the world of thought in which they lived. They have definite attributes, corresponding to definite qualities and functions, and these cannot be varied at will. Fortuna has her rudder, her globe, her wheel, and her horn of magic plenty; Victory has the wreath and palm, such as the earthly victor bears. Pax has her olive branch, Justice her scales, Virtus her spear and sword, Liberalitas her account board, Felicitas her magic wand, Salus her snake. Occasionally an attribute may be transferred from one virtue to another, but never without intention.

Either the virtues are so close to one another as to be able naturally to exchange emblems—for example, Pax and Felicitas, or Justice and Aequitas, or one borrows from another to express some unusual aspect of her character. Victory can by way of exception carry the branch of Pax to show that she herself is the bringer of peace, or, conversely, Pax can carry the palm of Victory to show that she herself comes out of triumph. The details are curious and elaborate and may be left to the specialists; the main point is easy to grasp and most important in its implications. The world of the virtues was no unordered chaos; its forms were relatively clear and stable, and when you entered it you found little room for arbitrary choice and caprice. The attenuated ghosts of personifications, which are all that survive today, make us forget how real the virtues once were to their worshipers.

Even in the ancient world there was a fringe of uncertainty surrounding the many familiar virtues. New figures might from time to time be added and might or might not establish themselves in current use, just as a language may grow new words and idioms. Thus we do find even in antiquity personifications, made for an occasion by poets and artists, that were not drawn from general belief and that never made their way into it. They had as little vitality as personifications today. The fact remains that this was the exception rather than the rule. Lucian has some excellent sport at the expense of such fancies when he makes Zeus summon a council of the gods to decide what is to be done about the many unauthorized newcomers who are appearing in Olympus without any credentials. Among these are such creatures as Hope and Faith, mere names of things that have not and could never have any real existence. But Lucian's satire goes too far and, as with most skeptics, reveals as much lack of understanding as presence of it.

The virtues, like the gods, were represented in human form. Again the question arises, was this representation taken as literally true? Or was it recognized as a mere conventional form of expression? The question may perplex us, but it is doubtful whether it would ever have perplexed the plain Roman. To him the spiritual world was remarkably substantial and solid. Tertullian, we may remember, is very sure that the soul itself is corporeal. The spiritual world is just the other side of the material world. In that world live the virtues, and from that world they are revealed to us in the forms in which we know them. Since these forms are constant, they may be taken as representing what the virtues are as expressed in an idiom that we can understand. What they may be apart from us is none of our concern—supposing it to have any meaning at all.

VI

Religion and the State: Emperor Worship

AFTER RELIGION came politics, for even in an authoritarian state like the Roman Empire the individual citizen could not be entirely shut off from an instinctive interest in his political surroundings. A natural bridge from the one to the other is provided by the special form of state religion that the Empire produced—the worship of the emperor.

In classical antiquity religion and politics stood normally in the closest relations to one another—even if that might only mean that religion was entirely subordinated to national interests. The Greek and Roman peoples, who found their fullest self-expression in the intense but restricted life of a city-state, drew the line between public and private life at a different point from ours. A very large part of the life of the Greek and Roman was spent in public—if not actually on public duty, in assembly or law courts, at least in public places, in the market or the gymnasium. The life of the home, to which woman was supposed to be restricted, was narrow in scope and interests; most of education and a good part of social intercourse fell outside its jurisdiction. It is only in accordance with this general trend that religion is found to have a strongly political character. Not that there were no private cults and no personal devotion. Both in Athens and Rome there were time-hallowed worships proper to the family; in both, many an individual felt the need for spiritual help and guidance. But the importance of private worship, compared to that of the state, was not rated very high, and there was a tendency to expect from everyone a general conformity to the religious traditions of the state. Socrates, though he himself endorsed the principle that you should worship the gods *nomoi poleos,* "after the custom of your states," was condemned to drink the hemlock for having introduced new gods and corrupted the youth! The real objection to the Epicureans, the charge that won them the opprobrious name of "atheists," was that they denied the active, busy gods who are ever mindful of the state. The ordinary Greek or Roman despised *apragmosyne,* withdrawal from affairs, in man, and he despised it equally in gods. Even in a Christian writer like Tertullian the same tendency sometimes appears as in the long diatribe against the heretic, Marcion. Tertullian has nothing but scorn for Marcion's second god, the good and gentle God of the New Testament, as opposed to the cruel, but just, Jehovah of the Old. Authority, he feels, can only really be benevolent (*philanthropos*) when it has compelled recognition of its strength—and the same principle holds good, both in heaven and on earth.

If we were right in interpreting the Roman view of the natural and spiritual worlds as always coexisting in intimate relation to one another, the state religion will appear as the other side of the state—the side that is turned towards the gods. The state cannot separate itself from them, and it is not in their nature to withdraw their interest from it. The possibility of disharmony between the two orders, natural and spiritual, was abhorrent to the Roman mind. If you were at peace with heaven, you expected health and prosperity as the natural fruits of that peace. The idea that the just and good might suffer, because they were just and good, was anything but congenial to the Roman.

The center of Roman state religion was the cult of the Capitoline triad, Jupiter, Juno, and Minerva. Jupiter, in particular, invoked as Optimus Maximus, was the recognized head of the Roman state. The goddess Roma was a late creation and her cult was found in Greece earlier than in Rome. The chief priestly offices always retained some of that political authority that from the first had been theirs in large measure, to say nothing of the abuses to which they lent themselves during the late Republic. When Augustus set his hand to the reform of the state, he found much to disquiet him in the state religion. Of the native simplicity and purity of the early belief much had been lost through too much experience of the world and through the subtle influence of Greek thought; there was a poverty of real devotion, a lack of tension everywhere that gave occasion for anxiety. But, if decline must be admitted, the nature of the decline should be clearly understood. There was no question of surrender to a religious rival, for no such rival yet existed. There was no question of a conscious and determined transition from religion to philosophy or scepticism. It was, in fact, little more than a general loss of tone due to discouragement and fatigue. The mood was not permanent. Augustus rebuilt temples and encouraged his poets to commend the old religion to his subjects. Reviving interest in religion would not flow only in the old channels; it sought new ones. The dream of a revival of the old Roman religion was only half capable of fulfillment. But the fatal apathy passed. Rome, the most religious of nations, had not attained Empire only to find herself incapable at the supreme moment of realizing her new experience in spiritual terms.

Rome was now the center of the civilized world. She had realized political unity; the demand for a religious unity soon followed. There was in this a strict logic for the Roman mind. The one body of the Empire must have one soul. Something could be done by allowing the provinces to share in the cults, which had once been purely Roman, something by attaching Greek and Roman names to gods of the provincials and equating them with Greek and Roman deities. But the demand really went beyond this; it was a demand for a god who could be universally recognized as the power behind the Empire and its emperor, a supreme and universal god. The most obvious claimant to the position was the Roman Jupiter, and, nominally at least, his claim was seldom contested. Yet for all that, no real imperial cult of Jupiter ever developed. In the third century, the sun-god for a moment almost succeeded where Jupiter had failed; Aurelian established Sol as "dominus imperii Romani" and set his worship beside that of the greatest gods in Rome. But in the long run the paganism that had proved itself so well adapted to the needs of city-state and country district failed in the new tasks set before it. The religion that was destined in the course of history to conquer the whole Empire was born in an obscure province and was slow to pass beyond the circles of the poor and oppressed. St. Paul, in his day, stood almost alone in his realization of the possibilities the future held for it.

There was one development that, while offering to supply the religion that the Empire as a whole needed, could still be grafted on to traditional forms of paganism: worship of the emperor. Suggestions of such a worship might be found in several distinct quarters. The ancient kingdoms of the East, Assyria, Babylon, Persia, had all been accustomed to set their kings above the common herd, in a specially close relation to the gods, and had paid them reverence in a form that could easily be mistaken for direct worship. The Egyptians went even further and paid divine honors, without reserve, to their pharaohs. The worship of men as gods may fairly be held to be repugnant to the pure Greek spirit; but at an early date that spirit began to suffer violence. Lysander the Spartan was the first Greek to receive divine honors. When Alexander the Great conquered Asia and succeeded to the position of King of Kings, he had the example ready at hand. He had risen above the limits of ordinary greatness, and this could best be acknowledged by calling him a god. To style this a fiction, invented for political use, is only partly to explain it. Behind it lay a genuine belief that there was something in the exceptional individual that went beyond ordinary humanity. The example of Alexander was followed by his successors—the Seleucids in Syria and Asia, the Ptolemies in Egypt, a country in itself inured to the idea of divinity in its rulers. Only the kings of Macedonia itself ruled as of old as men over men. In the East, generally, the conception of the god-king was firmly established. When Roman proconsuls succeeded as viceroys in countries long ruled by kings they found their subjects only too ready to pay similar honors to them. Partly from vanity, partly from policy, they made little difficulty about accepting these honors.

The Romans themselves had a strong sense of the gulf between god and man. Yet there was one root in their religion from which emperor worship might grow. The Romans paid tribute to the *di manes,* the spirits of the dead. The worship was chthonic—of the kind paid to the nether gods, not to the upper gods of light and sky—and it may have played a minor part in belief; but worship it certainly was, even though some modern scholars have been inclined to obscure the fact. Its influence on emperor worship may be seen in the special cult of the *divi,* the emperors deified after death.

To minds long trained in the enlightened teaching of monotheistic religion, there is, in this worship of the man-god, something indecent and absurd. To worship a man of the same flesh and blood as ourselves, to suppose him able to control the seasons or the tides because for a short span he held sway over the state, is surely as silly as it is wrong. There were not lacking even in antiquity occasional critics who saw clearly the silliness if not so much the wrongness. But there are several considerations that, if they do not excuse the worship of man, do make it more intelligible. The first is this, that the word "god" (*deus, theos*) had a very much wider meaning to a Greek or Roman than it has today. A name, which in its most proper use belongs only to the supreme ruler of the universe, was degraded to denote an emotion of the soul, the spirit of a place, even some individual man placed for the moment in a position of exceptional importance. A powerful friend, able to help you in your need, is a god to you. Once the debasement of the word had begun, it went on almost without limit. Again, as the word, "god," extended its meaning, two dis-

tinct classes of gods appear: the transcendental gods who op-
erate outside man in nature and the universe, and the imma-
nent gods who are manifested in and through him. When you
have once begun to worship the "inner gods," the virtues in a
man's soul, it is only one step further to worship the man himself. The special Roman belief in the genius, or spirit, of an
individual might also lead on towards worship; for the genius
was always recognized as something more permanent and reliable than the normal, fallible individual can be. Although
the worship of the emperor was not always limited in this
way—although he might be held up to honor as a numen, able
to express his will in the material world—it was certainly
through the cult of the imperial virtues that many men found
it possible to acquiesce in the cult of the emperor himself. In
early Christian writers one can find something of a similar
tendency to represent Jesus Christ as a special virtus, or power,
of God. It was decisively defeated when Athanasian orthodoxy triumphed over the heresy of Arius.

There was another movement in the later paganism usually
called after the name of its first great prophet, Euhemerus,
that was exactly the opposite of the one that we have been discussing. Instead of finding something of God in every man,
exalting man to heaven, it brought down even the greatest of
the gods to earth. The great gods universally worshiped, even
Jupiter (Zeus) himself, were originally men. They had lived
on earth, had fought and founded kingdoms, and when
they died they received divine honors as their reward from a
grateful posterity. In the case of some hero-gods—Liber,
Castor and Pollux, Hercules—the way of ascent was still remembered. But Jupiter himself had his tomb in Crete and a
temple on which was inscribed the record of his services to
man.

The doctrine of Euhemerus, appearing apparently so soon
after Alexander, is clearly in one sense a mere rationaliza-
tion of the prevailing bad habit of deifying kings. Saviors and
benefactors, you say, have been deified from the beginning; so,
as you give the sounding titles to your kings, you can add

godhead, too. To find a justification for paying extravagant honors to the king, you have to degrade the god. Although Euhemerus was not one of the great thinkers of the world, his importance in the later pagan thought is supreme. Once the idea of an advancement by promotion for merit from earth to heaven had taken firm root, it grew steadily in use as a most convenient form of thought; it could be used to explain in a rational form the traditional religion of the state—even more, it could serve as a sanction for the consecration of each new emperor, who for his meritorious services to the state was duly divinized by the senate.

There was one other tendency that ran parallel to Euhemerism and could easily blend with it. Fortuna, the goddess of incalculable caprice, was often worshiped as a sort of complement—or even alternative—to the providence of the gods. She might be conceived of as operating through particular individuals. One might speak of the Fortune of Sulla or the Fortune of Caesar. You might begin by worshiping the Fortune of Caesar and soon find yourself worshiping Caesar himself.

From such roots as these, set deep in custom and belief, a cult of the emperor could readily grow. But the actual course of development was largely determined by the emperors themselves, acting on certain broad principles and with conscious political intention. A purely spontaneous growth might have been of a quite different character. Augustus found in the Empire a genuine disposition to recognize his unique position by exceptional, even by divine, honors. To this he found no objection and authorized worship of his person in the provinces with little restriction. Normally this worship was in conjunction with the goddess Roma. It suited the wishes of the people; it provided a focus for loyalty; and it supplied, if not a religion of the Empire, a substitute for one. In the provinces, then, emperor worship was soon established, beginning in the East but passing on to the West with little delay. In Rome and Italy there was definite repugnance to worshiping a man as god—a repugnance based on religious and political grounds combined. To the Roman the deity (numen) was far removed from ordinary human personality, even if he could be pictured in human shape; and the eastern potentates, who were worshiped as gods, bore also the name of king, offensive from of old to a Roman ear. At the same time in Rome and Italy as in the provinces the unique position of the emperor needed some grounding and some acknowledgment. A compromise was found that proved entirely successful. During his lifetime, while he moved as a man among men, the emperor was not worshiped; the offerings made to his genius or spirit or to his virtues were not paid to him as a person, but to divine powers operating through him. He stood very near to the gods, as their chosen, and could be seen treading the same path of service that had led Hercules heavenwards. But as soon as he was dead the objections to worship lapsed. The emperor, whose political career received the official approval of the senate, was "consecrated," that is to say, made a god. He received the title of "divus," as well as temples, altars, sacrifices, priests—in fact, all the appointments of worship. The honor could even be extended beyond the emperor to members of the imperial family, and the father or son, the wife or daughter of an emperor might be created divus or diva, as the case might be. The divi were clearly removed from the mass of the *di manes,* the spirits of the departed. Their place was not with the lower powers, the *inferi,* but with the *superi,* the powers of the sky. The bad emperor alone, whose memory was condemned by the senate, was thrust down into the nether world. A few emperors of ambiguous fame or fortune were left in an uncertain limbo between hell and heaven.

Consecration, as we meet it in Rome, is a religious act strongly affected by political considerations; service to man on earth earns worship after death. But how, if at all, was the act to be explained? How justify the escape of the divus from the ordinary lot of mortality? No ancient interpretation, if such there was, has survived to help us to understand the theology of the new worship. But it is probable that, so far as the matter was thought out, the consecration was conceived of not as a resurrection of the spirit but as a translation of the whole man, body, soul, and spirit, to a new sphere, accompanied by some mysterious change of essence to suit him to his new sphere. Romulus, in early Roman legend, was thus "translated" and ceased to be found among men; a certain C. Julius Proculus actually saw him ascending in the form of an eagle. This model was applied to the emperor. Augustus, after his death, was seen by a clairvoyant senator ascending as Romulus had ascended, and the release of an eagle from the funeral pyre came to be a normal part of the ceremony of consecration. The coins, our chief source of information, clearly show the varying shades of belief. Sometimes the divus is represented as borne skyward on the back of an eagle; sometimes the eagle seems actually to represent him; sometimes he is shown throned like Jupiter in heavenly majesty. Of course difficulties might be raised. The body of the dead emperor had to be disposed of, and how was this consistent with theories of translation? In practice the difficulty seems to have been dealt with by completely separating the two ceremonies: first, disposal of the body—a concern of the emperor's nearest friends and relatives —then the grand public ceremony.

The consequences of consecration in general if not always in detail can be clearly seen. As divus, the emperor was enrolled among the gods of Rome and the Empire. A special fraternity of priests (*sodales*) under a chief priest (*flamen*) was allotted to his worship—honors that only great gods like Jupiter or Mars enjoyed. There were temples, altars, statues, wreaths, banquets, sacrifices, and processions. Men could offer vows to him and swear by his name. That almost everything must have been borrowed or adapted from the old state worship is obvious. The detail, mainly lost, must have been curious and interesting. For Augustus himself we can conjecture that some features of his worship as divus—in particular the attributes of radiate crown, star, and thunderbolt—were borrowed from the special worship of the god Vediovis by the Julian "gens" at Bovillae. The fact of main importance is this: the deified emperor was worshiped with all the normal forms of pagan cult; no distinction to his disadvantage was made between him and the old gods. (Yet he is rather carefully called divus, not deus.)

If we would understand emperor worship as practised in the Roman Empire, we must get rid of some modern prejudices. Opposition to it there certainly was, but it came mainly from the Jews and the Christians. The plain man did not find it either absurd or base. The religion of the state was only the other side of the life of the state. The ruler of the state must stand nearer the gods than the ordinary man. Mortals had been raised before now from earth to heaven in reward for service to humanity. There were those, like Euhemerus, who said that there had never been any other way to heaven. What is so surprising, then, if this was still to be seen happening? So much for any supposed absurdity of the new worship, but what of its baseness? A partial answer has already been given. It is not base to worship a benefactor or savior, whereas it would be to worship a tyrant—and all the stress now falls on the goodness of the emperor. But one has to admit that the imagination of men was dazzled and blinded by the rise of the individual to positions of unique privilege and power, where he had almost universal power to hurt or to help. Men are moved, not only by mere self-interest but by a veritable passion for self-abasement, to humble themselves before the lord and exalt him sky-high. How terribly natural this humiliation can become our own generation is relearning to its cost.

What was to be the effect of the new cult on the old forms of pagan worship? Certainly there was no hostile intention of the new towards the old. It borrowed their forms and ceremonies and knit close bonds of relationship with them. But so far as the new had vitality it grew at the expense of the old, and the old polytheism, where it was still vigorous, lived in close association with the imperial cult. The gods are freely used as patterns or examples of the emperor—first in his lifetime, but more openly and freely after his death. The epithet, "Augustus," often applied to a god, links him closely to the emperor and his house. As time went on the relation of the gods to the emperor came to be more clearly defined, mainly under the two conceptions of *comites* and *conservatores*. The gods from their heaven look down and care for men. How better can they exercise their care than by following with their counsel and protection the emperor, to whom all men look for aid, who is already in life so close to the gods and who one day will join their number? It is most interesting to note that the gods tend to sink in dignity in relation to the emperor. The function of "comes" is important and honorable, but it is that of a subordinate at court, the companion or count. Conservator, in itself, is dignified enough; it can be associated with a type that shows a gigantic Jupiter stretching out the right hand of protection over a diminutive emperor. But the many "dei conservatores" of the third century remind us rather of the imperial bodyguard, or "protectores," chosen for fidelity and valor but of no specially high standing. The emperor was slowly acquiring a spiritual supremacy to balance the political. From the beginning of the Empire, the emperor might be associated in the worship of the gods, when vows were paid to them "pro salute Augusti." By the third century it is likely that almost all public worship had its political side; political loyalty and spiritual devotion are expressed by one and the same act.

Consecration, as we have seen, only came after death. "Sit divu dum non vivus" ("Let him be a god, as long as he is not a living man") was the brutal comment attributed to Caracalla when someone suggested that his murdered brother Geta be consecrated. Even in his lifetime the emperor enjoyed honors that lifted him high above his fellow men. Libations to his genius were poured on every suitable occasion, and worship was paid to his virtues, the divine powers of good that operated in him. These could be almost as varied and manifold as life itself. A few will serve as patterns of the rest. Most important of all, perhaps, is Victoria Augusti, the inherent power to conquer. Close to her comes Virtus, courage and manly vigor, with which the emperor beats down his enemies. A possessor of Victoria and Virtus, the emperor is drawn very near to Jupiter, to whom the two goddesses are ministers. Of vital importance is Pax Augusti, the active spirit of the Pax Augusta—no vague personification, no passivity of mind, but a power working through the emperor to enforce peace abroad and to maintain it at home. Pax is the converse and companion of Virtus; the Empire rests in a nice balance between the two. Providentia might well have been selected as the cardinal imperial virtue, but this was certainly not the case; she ranks below Victoria and no higher than Virtus and one or two others. One can see a reason likely to account for this. The pagan saw the world under the aspect of Fortuna as well as of Providentia, as the sport of blind chance as well as the servant of unchanging law. Whichever of the two views you chose, the position of the emperor remained unique, but you attributed it to Fortuna Augusti in the one view, to Providentia Augusti or Providentia Deorum in the other. Providentia Augusti brings the emperor near to that providence that belongs not to Jupiter but to the whole divine order, Providentia Deorum, as one aspect perhaps of that law of destiny that even the gods obey. Felicitas Augusti, a close companion of Pax, is the happiness or luck of the emperor, not merely a state but a virtue that begins with him and can extend from him by a kind of happy contagion to all who come into contact with him. One more virtue—decidedly less common—may be mentioned, Aeternitas Augusti. Aeternitas cannot be interpreted as a mere description of the triumph of the imperial office over time. She is an indwelling spirit, proper to the man who after death is to join the gods in the eternal sphere. She links the emperor to the thought of eternal Rome and to the mystical conceptions lying behind such terms as the "Great Year" and the "Restoration of the Times."

Such in its outlines was the worship of the god-man—the supreme symbol of the world-state. What was its meaning and value to the Romans? There can be no single answer—only a series of answers, varying with the time and varying also with the class. Until well into the third century the importance of emperor worship was steadily increasing, until it reached a peak under Trajan Decius. From then on it did not so much decay as suffer a change of direction. Something very vigorous and alive was needed to meet the challenge of the Christian Church and the pressure of an iron age. It was to the living, not to the dead, that Rome turned for salvation. The living emperor must stand out as the favored champion of the world order, with the whole host of heaven alert to guide and defend him, or he must be brought into some very intimate relation with the great gods. If Romans cannot actually rank him as a god, he must be brought as near godhead as possible. Thus Diocletian, if not actually Jupiter, becomes Jovius, the special favorite of Jupiter—perhaps even more, the man whose genius is derived from the supreme god himself. Thus, too, Maximian becomes, if not Hercules, at least Herculius and can adapt the labors of the hero-god as emblems of his own work. The final solution—the substitution of divine right for divinity—will concern us later.

It remains to see how belief might vary with class and status. The Roman nobles, except to the limited extent to which they were caught up in the imperial government, were inclined to hold themselves aloof. They reckoned themselves to be the peers of the emperor and found it slightly absurd that divine honors should be paid to one who might even be below them in social rank. Yet the senate as a body accepted the new rite. It met the need of a religion for the Empire and served as a focus for the very real devotion that the wonderful organism of Roman government won. The knights—the second order of the nobility—were in general the emperor's men; they depended largely on his favor for the interesting and lucrative careers now open to them. The army accepted emperor worship as an easy and natural form of expressing loyalty. The honor of the profession and its emoluments and privileges hung upon the emperor: in honoring him, the army honored itself. The freedmen were cunningly won over to the new religion by the creation of the order of "Augustales," which was designed especially for them and which found its life in the public ceremonies of emperor worship. The lower class accepted it with resignation, if not always with enthusiasm. The emperor was their patron, they looked to him for protection and for the satisfaction of their needs; they could not always be remembering the little things—liberty, for example —that he took away. The provincials were proud of the new badge of servitude; the peace and security of the Empire were well worth the price. The rich found occupation and enhanced reputation in the holding of the imperial priesthoods. The great cities fought for such a title as "templekeeper" of the imperial cult. The poor could feel for themselves the political if not the religious meaning of the new system. There is some definite evidence, apart from general probability, that some simple souls actually accepted the divi as powers capable of answering prayer.

Emperor worship, then, was to a large extent successful. It fulfilled the purposes for which it was first devised. It did not run to wild and ridiculous excesses; it acquired a certain dignity and authority, as of a long accepted convention. But its success was strictly limited; it never became—never looked as if it would become—a religion of the heart for the whole Empire. Religion was becoming more democratic. The plain man was no longer satisfied with the religion of the old aristocracy, the religion of the state. The individual was claiming attention as never before. As he ceased to count in politics, except as a cypher, to escape inanition he sought to express himself in religion. Nor were his claims simply personal and selfish—for more pleasure and security for himself to enjoy. There was a deep desire for the enhancement of value in personal life—the desire in fact for righteousness, and to all this the worship of the emperor had not one word to say.

Emperor worship, then, for all its show of success, lacked a solid basis. It was readily accepted among the conventions of life; the virtues of the living emperors and the memory of the divi were freely recorded on the coins, but it was not so easy to gain access to men's hearts. Of open opposition there was little. The purely religious objection, that honors proper to the gods are assigned to men, is very seldom heard. The devout pagan seems hardly to have felt it. The philosophers, of course, had their doubts and discreetly expressed them—more often in the safety of limited private circles than in harangues to the mob. Philosophy had its martyrs, but they were usually political, not religious. To the mocking skeptic Lucian, emperor worship must have seemed as absurd as the rest of paganism, but he did not look for trouble by singling it out for attack. Effective resistance was really left to those religious minorities that had strength in themselves to refuse the easy tolerations of paganism—the Jew, with his stern monotheism, and the Christian, with his equally stern insistence on the worship of the One True God, revealed in Jesus Christ. The doctrine of the Trinity was not fully developed until the fourth century, and a pagan observer of early Christianity might have imagined that the Christians worshiped two or even three gods. The Jew, too, would chide the Christian for what he termed his defection from monotheism. For all that chiding, Jew and Christian stood very close together in their opposition to the worship of the emperor.

With the Jew, opposition was often political as well as religious, if one may attempt to report two strands in what often seems to blend in one. The Romans had learned to recognize and respect the peculiar prejudices of the Jews and, in theory, carried toleration up to the limits of possibility. Caligula proposed to compel the Jews to worship him, but, to the relief of Romans as well as of Jews, he died without carrying out his threat. In the end, the combination of religious nonconformity with stiff national pride and love of independence proved too strong for all attempts at reconciliation. Jerusalem was stormed and the temple destroyed by Titus. Two generations later Hadrian desecrated the sacred site by founding his pagan colony there. Some degree of toleration was still enjoyed by the Jews, individually and in their smaller groups, but it was granted more of necessity than of good will. It was in fact forced on any government that was not willing to go to the other extreme of extermination.

With the Christians, opposition was almost purely religious. The early Church regarded the Empire as friend rather than enemy, and even the persecutions of Nero and Domitian could not quite destroy that initial feeling. True, the position of the Church was precarious; it could always be treated as an unauthorized society, a "collegium illicitum." But persecution, though always threatening, might for long be held off. The government did not seek out the Christians and refused to receive anonymous denunciations of them. It was felt to be worthwhile laying the Christian case before the emperor and demonstrating to him that the Christians were not guilty of the enormities commonly attributed to them. Loyal the Christians certainly were. They learned from their teachers to respect lawful authority, they saw in the Roman Empire the one bulwark maintained by divine providence to delay the coming of antichrist. They were disinclined to take part in civil war, and they prayed with a single heart for the preservation of the emperor. They prayed, however, not to the many gods of the heathen, not to men who had been made gods, but to the One Father of men in heaven. They asserted in practice that common sense about what the divine can and cannot be, which was largely admitted in theory by the better pagan thinkers but hidden by a conspiracy of silence.

How the latent antagonism of Empire and Church grew to open and violent clash is well known. There were two points of view, which could never be completely reconciled. The Empire was "totalitarian"; the Church obeyed, but with its own reservations. As the Church grew in numbers, in influence, in self-knowledge, and self-confidence, and, one must in honesty add, in worldliness, it lost its early millennial dream. It came to realize that it must live in and with the Empire, not for a very brief "last time" but for an indefinitely long future. There were several stages of conflict, interrupted by working compromises only partially successful. The Church had at first been obscure and despised and was persecuted at irregular intervals of time and place, more as a measure of policies than of politics. During the second century it enjoyed a large measure of toleration. Christians were known in private to be decent and law-abiding citizens, for all that they bore the black mark of membership in an unauthorized society. Early in the third century a new phase set in. The Empire for the first time began to lose its nerve under the shadow of recurrent disasters and to fear its rival, the growing Church; the society that had been a mere nuisance was now felt to be a public danger. The persecutions of Trajan Decius and Valerian failed to crush the Church, and the "peace" of Gallienus gave it breathing space. But the peace lacked sure foundations and was in fact an armistice rather than a peace. The great persecution, set on foot by Diocletian and Galerius, marked the final failure of the policy of repression. The Church, though maimed and broken, still lived on. It only remained for Constantine to conclude a real peace with the Church and to allot to it, if not the immediate possession, at least the reversion to the rank of state religion. In the New Rome become Christian, Church and state were to run in harness. The only question was, which partner was to predominate. Constantine, by his strong gifts of character and his mingling of favor and firmness, brought the Church into a condition of almost complete submission to his will. In the eastern Empire, the balance of power remained on the political side. In the west, the Church triumphed, but only because the state, its partner, collapsed.

With the victory of Christianity, emperor worship as an institution was bound to go, even if some lingering traces of it can be seen as late as the death of Theodosius the Great. But an equivalent for it was soon found. The Church could recognize the emperor as the chosen of God, marked out by Him for his great office—distinct from and superior, but comparable to that of the bishops. The hand of God set the diadem on his head, the angel Victory guarded his throne, and when he died one might say that the chariot of the Lord was sent to fetch him, as it had been sent for Elijah. How much was in fact retained, how much changed? How hard it always is to gauge what happens when some revolutionary force has exhausted its initial momentum and, in contact with all that makes for conservatism, enters on a new stabilization! To pursue this question, we should have to leave the ancient world behind and follow the track to the Middle Age.

VII

State and Citizen

THE WORLD of the Roman Empire was undoubtedly weary of politics. It was ready, for the bribe of peace, to leave all the responsibilities and all the prizes to others. Yet politics comprises so large a part of life that it is impossible, with the best will in the world, to cancel all interest in it. Even under the Roman Empire man continued to be a "political animal."

What in its essential nature was the Roman Imperial Government? An autocracy certainly, for, however the fact might be masked by convenient pretences, the real power was concentrated in the hands of a single man. One might even call it a military autocracy on the ground that it rested ultimately on the support of the army. It had its constitutional side; to be fully legitimate an emperor needed the approval of the senate. But fact was more powerful than theory. It was easier to legitimize an irregular *fait accompli* than to enforce a just claim that lacked military support. Moreover, wherever the power was finally vested, whether in the emperor himself, in his chief lieutenants and civil servants, in the senate, or in the army, the state was supreme. Every state, even the humblest, can if needed assert its absolute right to the obedience of its citizens. But in the Roman Empire the scale was so vast, the concentration of power in the executive so extreme, that the ordinary man was helpless, morally and physically, before it. To ensure stability, the Roman had forged for himself an instrument of terrifying power.

The Roman Empire was definitely based on the principle of authority; the rights of the state, the duties of the subject were emphasized. A democratic government, resting on the support of the people, naturally puts their interests in the foreground. Where purely material things such as corn or games are concerned, the ordinary man sees little difference what kind of government gives them to him; the gift is the important thing, the label attached to it a matter of taste. But when you pass from the material to things that you cannot weigh and measure, to the rights summed up in the one word, "liberty," the difference between the two types of state becomes apparent. The democrat will claim certain forms of freedom—freedom of speech, for example—as his natural right. The autocrat knows of no such natural rights in fact of the state; it is only the state that can judge what is suitable in each case. On the one side lies license, on the other tyranny.

But if the Roman Empire was very strong and very autocratic we must not be in a hurry to attach to it our modern label "totalitarian state." For all the analogies that it presents to the painful, if interesting, experiments of modern Europe, it was in many ways far different from them. In its theoretical claims it was like enough. It was ready to reduce everyone to one level of subordination and to refuse to allow any department of life to claim exemption from its scrutiny. It might tolerate religions other than that of the state as a matter of policy, but it issued no general edict of toleration. In actual fact, for some three centuries it did not realize its latent possibilities. We may call it a totalitarian state in a condition of arrested development. In the fourth century the case changed, if not quite as abruptly as our scanty records suggest, yet abruptly enough. The Empire was bankrupt at home and gravely embarrassed on every frontier; it was only at the cost of a merciless overhauling that the whole machine was saved from destruction. The state, under the "new order" of Diocletian and Constantine, claimed to have a finger in every pie, to supervise everything, to spy on everyone. It laid the foundations of the Byzantine Empire in the east; even in the west it gave Roman civilization a few more generations to live. But it was an ugly system, born of emergency, often wasteful and unintelligent, threatened with destruction from its uncorrected evils, foreign and domestic, its inflated bureaucracy, and its hopeless and merciless system of taxation. Even under the early Empire the grip of imperial rule seems to have begun to paralyze the nerve of invention in literature and art. That the inspirations of the Republic should have fallen mute is no just cause for surprise or complaint. But a healthy Empire might have been expected in time to find voices of power to express its meaning and shape its hopes for the future. It is not altogether a healthy sign that for the praises of the Empire we have to look very largely to the occasional testimony of the poor and lowly.

There are two distinct aspects of the Roman Empire: the official and juristic (the account given by statesmen and constitutional lawyers) and the popular (the way in which it worked out in practice for the man in the street). The juristic view might be variously stated at different times, but it amounted to something like this. The Roman state, i.e., the senate and people of Rome (the senate being now the political representative of the people) continues to exist and appoint magistrates as of old to carry out its business, but owing to the vast extent of the Empire and the mass and complication of public affairs, it has become necessary to appoint a special magistrate, i.e., emperor, with powers built up out of a number of republican offices to coördinate the whole and, especially, to hold in firm control the army, on which in the last resort the government depends. The state is still supreme, the emperor, in theory, no more than its representative, but the delegation of power is so thorough that it is as good as impossible to demand account from an emperor, except by deposition, which usually means death. The support of the army is always an absolute essential; in times of crisis it can intervene to overthrow an emperor or to choose between rival claimants for the vacant position. A very great scholar, Mommsen, has tried to translate these facts into a form of constitution. The army is the last surviving representative in politics of the "populus Romanus." It has a right equal to that of the senate to create an emperor, but it does so in its own way; it hails him as "imperator," whereas the senate passes a decree, conferring the imperial power. If this were really the case, as Mommsen thought, the Roman Empire lived and chose to live under the constant shadow of revolution. No one could tell which form of election, the civil or the military, would on any one occasion prevail. It is quite possible that Mommsen's theory would have found support in the ranks of the Roman army, could it have been expounded to them. The civilian population certainly chose to regard election by the senate as the normal procedure, military interference as a painful accident.

The juristic view of the Empire probably interests modern scholars far more than it ever interested the ancient world. Even men of affairs may have been content to note the various ways in which things were done without converting them into a system. Augustus and his advisers, by way of experiment, inaugurated a form of government that proved capable of working and settled down to be permanent. Its later development was determined less by great bills of reform than by the vast series of imperial acts that kept on establishing ever new precedents. No ancient writer has given us in full his theory of the imperial constitution. The nearest to it that we have is the sketch of the ideal Empire suggested by Maecenas to Augustus in the pages of Dio Cassius. In the political world, no doubt, the fact usually comes first; the constitution is only its reflection. But in Rome there was a good and sufficient reason for not defining the Empire too closely. It was an autocracy, disguised under constitutional forms, and the disguise was less easy to penetrate if the forms were purposely left vague.

For our present study it is the popular, the practical view of the Empire alone that seriously matters, for it was that that determined the the attitude of the public towards the emperor. The emperor was familiar to the people of Rome as the master of the army—for even in Rome he had his imperial prae-

torians—as the giver of bread and games, "panem et cir-
censes," as the chief initiator of legislation in the senate, as the
most influential patron at election. On the obverse of the coins,
where the head of some tutelary deity had once stood, the
Roman citizen now saw the features of the emperor. Many
rites and ceremonies proper to royal courts began to be
assigned to the emperor and his family. The Roman would
not call him either god or king, but the Greek world, and in
fact the provinces at large, did not grudge either title. To the
constitutional lawyer, the emperor was defined as "imperator,
tribunicia potestate, pontifex maximus, pater patriae." To the
ordinary man he was well on the way to being a god-king—
and the ordinary man was nearer to the facts of the case than
the constitutional lawyer.

The first great fact in the popular view was the acceptance
of the autocracy of a single man. There was always the danger
of tyranny, if the autocrat used his powers ignorantly and un-
wisely to the injury of his subjects or corruptly to gratify his
own desires; but he was needed and the risk had to be run.
Supreme power, however, can be used as well as abused. In
the east men had long been familiar with the conception of a
king who is the channel through which all blessings flow to
his people. This idea was now taken up by rhetoricians and
philosophers, and fancy pictures were drawn of what a perfect
emperor might be expected to be. It has been observed, with
much justice, that this was one of the few means of political
criticism that still remained available; in sketching your ideal
ruler you might convey hints or even warnings to the emperor
himself. A Greek would write of the virtues of the perfect
king (*basileus*), avoiding the word "tyrant" (*tyrannos*)
with its suggestions of illegality. A Roman would avoid the
offensive word "king" and would as a rule pass over even the
less offensive "imperator." He preferred the vague but convenient word *princeps,* chief citizen, and would seek in an
"optimus princeps" the perfect ruler of a perfect state
(*optimus status rerum*)—a condition in which all parts of
the constitution worked in harmony to the advantage of the

whole. The panegyric delivered by the Younger Pliny before
the Emperor Trajan is a fine example of this class of composition. It skillfully blends praise of the emperor for what he is
with tactful suggestions as to what so good a man will find it
suitable to do in future and with a few guarded warnings as
to what he would do well to avoid. Jupiter Optimus Maximus
is the official protector of Rome; the "optimus status," then,
will be chiefly his concern. The "optimus princeps," who can
contribute more than anyone else to the perfect state, is Jupiter's chief gift to Rome and stands under his immediate and
constant protection.

What this excellence of prince and state might be expected
to imply will become clearer, as we analyze some of the chief
ideas that were caught up into it. The "best of princes" must
be pious in his service of the gods, just in his dealings with his
subjects, strong and victorious in face of the enemy, but merciful after victory; he must be temperate and kind, and—a characteristic ancient trait—liberal. He must love peace and concord, those precious gifts without which states collapse into
decay. Inscriptions of honor and, far above all else, the succession of imperial coins give us very vivid impressions of the
"optimus princeps" and the "optimus status" as conceived at
different times. The form of expression employed is the celebration of the virtues that govern the chief activities of the
emperor. For, though such celebration moves partly in the
world of fact and bears witness to actual achievement, it tends
to move out beyond this into a realm of hope and promise.
Sometimes, when times are bad, it seems to be all promise and
no achievement.

The imperial virtues were many and were always tending to
increase in number. Abundantia, Aequitas, Clementia, Concordia, Felicitas, Fides, Hilaritas, Justitia, Laetitia, Liberalitas,
Libertas, Moneta, Munificentia, Pax, Pietas, Providentia, Salus,
Spes, Tranquillitas, Ubertas, Victoria, Virtus—the names come
readily to the pen, and the list could be indefinitely extended.
We shall have occasion a little later to examine the characteristics of some of the most important of them. Apart from any

ideal considerations, the emperor was important to his subjects for the protection of life and property that he provided, for the corn that he supplied free or at a low price, for the games and shows with which he enlivened the leisure of the capital. There can be no doubt of the sincere acceptance, even the enthusiastic acceptance, of the "ruler" principle. If the ruler was to be controlled, it was to be rather by the force of sound precepts and examples working on his noble nature than by external force.

On the political side the position of the emperor was based on the free consent of his people. As token of this, he bore the tribunitian power, which constituted him the sacrosanct defender of the people's rights and conferred, or at least carried with it, a number of special powers. The emperor worked in the closest possible association with the senate, the political representative of the Roman people. The force to back up his authority was assured to him by the supreme command of the army. It was to the emperor that the soldier owed allegiance, from the emperor that he drew his pay. The first emperor had risen to power as the head of a party or faction in the state. But it was obviously undesirable that this view of his position should become permanent. If he was always to remain the powerful patron from whom his clients might expect substantial and material benefits as the price of their support, he was no longer a party chief; all loyal citizens could join his clientele. As we saw in the last chapter, the emperor, though not a god-king like the rulers of the Hellenistic East, could yet enjoy honors approaching the divine in his lifetime and could look forward to consecration as the reward of a virtuous reign. Without question men attached to his rule some kind of divine sanction, some grace of the gods, a grace sometimes described in modern books by the somewhat vague and mystical word "charisma." More than one shade of meaning struggles here for mastery. It was probably the political aspect that dominated; the divine grace was attached rather to the office than to the person of the emperor. But a more personal interpretation was not excluded and was always likely to encroach

on the purely political. A chosen house, or even a chosen individual, might seem to draw to itself in an unusual degree that
grace of heaven. Disturbance of the succession was one of the
evils most to be dreaded. Stability was the great need of the
many, disputed succession could at best benefit the few. Stren-
uous attempts were made to ensure it by letting son succeed
father or by moving the emperor to mark out by adoption the
man he judged best suited to succeed him. The "providence of
the Gods," presiding over the whole course of Empire, was invoked to add a religious sanction to the political design.

Let us now see how the various benefits and services the
Roman citizen hoped to enjoy from the emperor were
grouped under the imperial virtues. The emperor must be
strong and victorious; otherwise he will not be emperor long.
He must be attended by Virtus and Victoria. Clementia, the
gentler virtue that balances Virtus, will teach him to be merciful, where mercy is in place. Pax will make him "pacifer," a
bearer of peace at home and abroad. The emperor has vast
material resources at his disposal, and it is vital that he should
use them for the good of his people. Abundantia, Annona, and
Ubertas are the powers that guide him in handling supplies.
Aequitas is seen in the fair management of the corn supply,
Liberalitas in the distribution of largesse to citizens, Munificentia in generous provision for the shows of the arena.
Moneta, the spirit of the imperial mint, guides the emperor in
the control of his coinage, especially as paymaster general of
the troops. Fortuna bestows the imperial rank. Felicitas lends
a happiness that passes on from the emperor to others; Salus
preserves the emperor that he may preserve the state. Providentia inspires him with wise care for his subjects, whether in
planning the state budget, in dealing with usurpers, or in de-
termining the succession. Libertas, the spirit of liberty, the
spirit of the old Republic, lives on, restricted in scope but still
the defender of the freedom of the subject and enemy of
tyranny. Concordia is that harmony in virtue of which alone
the state can exist; she finds her special seat in the emperor
who, as the city mob shouted to Vitellius when he spoke of

abdicating and hanging up his dagger in the temple of Concord, "himself is Concord." Securitas, like Salus, begins with the emperor and radiates out from him, giving freedom from anxiety about domestic and foreign dangers. Hilaritas and Laetitia suggest the glow of happiness that the whole state shares on such auspicious occasions as marriages or births in the imperial family. Aeternitas links the emperor to Roma Aeterna and her limitless destiny, while Spes, looking forward to the future, marks him as the chief surety for the hopes of his subjects. Many other virtues—Justitia, Indulgentia, Patientia, Tranquillitas, and the rest—fill in the picture of a background of joy and prosperity.

Concordia is a virtue who reigns over a very wide kingdom. She gives harmony in the imperial family, harmony in the state between emperor and senate, harmony in the army. If her care is once relaxed, Rome becomes the victim of struggles between competing persons and classes. She is the soul of the imperial peace, which, if it must be on the one hand defended by Victoria and Virtus, on the other needs the gentler care of Concordia. It is easy to take a cynical view when one sees what ugly realities were sometimes veiled by the pleasant word. But the Concordia of the Empire was certainly a very real force; she meant the willing coöperation of the subject in the great imperial scheme. It was not always when her blessings were most realized that we hear most about her. "Concordia exercituum" under the early Empire was very commonly realized, comparatively rarely advertised. The harping on this theme in the coinage of the third century is a direct evidence of the military anarchy.

Fides again was a virtue of wide range and capital importance. As between ruler and subject she has two distinct sides. She prompts the loyalty that the subject owes his ruler, the protection that he may expect in return. Fides, again, is the special loyalty owed by the soldier to the general, "into whose words" he has sworn—to whom he has sworn allegiance. The goddess Fides is constantly invoked, as was Concordia, in face of the terrible soldier mob of the third century. The symbol of the clasped hands applies equally to all these relationships.

Pietas is the most Roman of all the virtues and the most difficult for the modern mind to understand. There is no single English word that will cover all her meanings. "Piety" corresponds roughly if not exactly to a part, "pity" to another part. Where the word pietas is used in its widest sense, "goodness" is our nearest English equivalent. Pietas implies readiness to act rightly in all cases where obligation exists, and, like Fides, often expresses the reciprocal relationship between two parties. To the Roman she was the cardinal virtue; the scrupulous care for covenanted duties was to him more valuable than romantic devotion or chivalrous generosity. Duty is owed first of all to the gods. This is piety in the religious sense, never quite excluded by other shades of meaning, for duty to the gods can be held to include in itself all minor duties. Duty to parents, children, and kindred comes very close after. The good man must not be wanting in proper respect for his closest natural ties. There is a special Pietas applicable to dependents and clients, for between them and the patron there exists a relationship governed by exact laws. Towards others, strangers at home or abroad, Pietas does not at first extend, for they are outside the covenant; but the stranger at home may be admitted to clientship, the enemy abroad to grace, and Pietas, now very near in meaning to "pity," pleads for his admission. A contemporary, hearing the story of Dido betrayed by Aeneas, curls the lip at a hero who can behave so meanly. But Dido herself never calls Aeneas, her faithless lover, "impius," and the Roman could pity Dido without blaming Aeneas as we do. It mattered to him much more than it does to us that Aeneas had deliberately refrained from binding himself by the ties to which pietas is attached. If he could in any sense be termed "impius," it would be for his ingratitude to his benefactress rather than for his cruelty to his love. A virtue so wide in scope as pietas was admirably suited to sum up the character of a virtuous emperor and the Romans honored Antoninus Pius much as Englishmen honored Victoria "the Good." Something was lost, when the title Pius, combined with Felix, was stereotyped as part of the imperial style and the emperor could begin at once to enjoy a reputation without first earning it.

Libertas is a virtue that interests us most closely today. She seems to us the vital spirit of any state that is worth living and dying for. Under the Roman Empire her range was sadly limited. Even the best of emperors could not pretend that he could offer liberty in the old sense, and it was not every emperor who cared to remember that he was but the trustee for the rights of his subjects. Trajan, on one occasion when he called in the old republican coinage, reissued a number of types as his own restorations, and by his choice emphasized the fact that the Empire was the direct descendant of the free Republic. He honored even the memory of Brutus the "liberator," one of the murderers of Julius Caesar. But the old constitution, if not dead, was changed out of all recognition. The people no longer elected the magistrates—that right had passed to the senate—and even the senate was in fact terribly weak when faced with the immense powers concentrated in the hands of the emperor. Liberty, in the purely political sense, hardly existed. So far as the word still had meaning, liberty looked to the personal rights of the citizen which a good emperor would still respect—the right to freedom from wanton interference by the police or arbitrary and unnecessary increases of taxation. When the possession of Empire was in doubt, both parties naturally made their appeal to Libertas. The pretender would claim to be championing Libertas against a tyrant. The reigning emperor, if he succeeded in overthrowing the usurper, might boast of "Libertas Restituta," constitutionalism asserted against revolution. By a curious turn of thought, assisted by verbal similarity, Libertas was often associated with Liberalitas. The emperor's free spirit showed itself in freeness in giving. One of the chief advantages of Libertas to our plain Roman was his share in the imperial largesses. Caracalla's extension of Roman citizenship over the whole Empire was naturally celebrated under the same title.

Some virtues there were that were most commonly assigned to ladies of the imperial family. As might be expected, these looked more to private than to public life. Such, for example, was Fecunditas, the virtue of the good wife and mother. But other virtues too—Concordia, Felicitas, Pietas—could be specially related to the life of the imperial house. Pietas, aside from her reference to family affection, was proper to the empress, who, as wife of the Pontifex Maximus, had an important part to play in the religious life of the state.

If we look away from the emperor, there is only one other feature of importance left in public life—the senate. Elections of magistrates, political meetings—all are gone; the state is as dead politically as in recent Germany or Italy. Almost everything that is done is traceable at once either to the emperor or to the mass of deputies who carry out his will. The senate, however, continued to take a definite share in government, partly by itself, partly in collaboration with the emperor. Rome and Italy and the more peaceful provinces were at least partially under its control. Although the emperor had some rights of nomination and recommendation, the senate elected the magistrates. Although the emperor struck gold and silver coin, the senate signed the bulk of the token money of brass and copper with its own mark, S.C., *Senatus Consulto,* "by decree of the Senate." Many of the emperor's own measures were put into force through decrees of the senate, when, in virtue of his tribunitian power, he had referred them to it as propositions. The prestige of the senate continued to rank high till halfway through the third century. It was the link with the past and the security against tyranny in the present. Many an emperor chose to pay homage on the coinage to the genius of the senate and to boast of his own concord with that body. Had the senate as a whole maintained a higher sense of its responsibilities, above all had it more consistently shown the courage it could muster up in emergency, its influence on the life of the Empire might have been even deeper and more salutary than it actually was.

The picture of the state that has emerged is clear and interesting. The rule of one man, virtually supreme, is accepted as an axiom. To the ordinary citizen he *is* the state. All its deepest and most permanent needs, strength and victory, abundance and prosperity, faith and piety, health and happiness, are bound up in his person. The senate has its place beside the emperor; it may even in an emergency rise to the top, but its normal role is severely restricted. Peace is the boon that is most steadily and fervently desired, for on it depend such possibilities of the good life as the Empire can still offer. Liberty is still valued, but no longer as the supreme good; it is never for long in the foreground. This is no unfair picture of the Roman Empire; even in it some good points are stressed, some bad points toned down. The Empire gave stability and rest to a weary and aging world. It demanded a high price, but it did not defraud its clients of their share in the bargain. If we look only at the outer, the political, aspect of the Empire we cannot assign it a very high place in history. At the best, it painfully conserves values already acquired; it does very little to acquire new ones. But if we look at the Empire from the inside we must award higher praise. It at least made a good life possible for many for whom it had been impossible before. If that possibility was not very widely realized, the blame lies less with the imperial government than with certain maladies of the age at which we must glance in a later chapter.

Our next chapter, "Peace and War," will show the Roman in relation to the world outside the Empire. But how did the Roman stand inside the Empire itself in relation to the provincials round him? Did he claim a special privilege, and did he claim it as his in perpetuity? At first, beyond all question, Rome was queen. Italy, under Julius Caesar, had been finally admitted to full partnership and shared it in increasing measure. But in the provinces Roman citizenship was only cautiously extended, and Roman forms of civic government only slowly encroached on local. In the end the distinction between Roman and subject faded until it was at last forgotten. The Empire became the inheritance of all its subjects. But there was something still amiss in what looks so happy an ending.

Privilege was jealously guarded, while it still had great value; it was only given freely, when the value was dwindling. There was a fatal weakness in the life of the provinces; there was no adequate provision for the expression of local opinion; there was no thought of altering the base on which the whole system rested. Even in its days of health the Empire lacked any vigorous principle of growth. When it fell on days of disease and misfortune, it developed maladies, any one of which might have been enough to kill it, even if we find it hard today to select the one that actually was responsible.

VIII

Peace and War

"Peace and war" is certainly the right order of words for the Roman Empire, not "War and Peace," as in the title of Tolstoy's great novel. Nearly twenty centuries after Augustus the world is still torn between the two. Despite the natural leaning of civilized man towards peace, war is still with us—a terrible source of suffering and evil, but a powerful solvent of old accretions. The world finds it equally impossible to live with it or without it. But the face of the Roman Empire was definitely set toward peace. For the subject peoples, peace was the splendid prize for which the high price of liberty had been paid. For the dominant Roman, peace was the crown of world victory. Had he been soldier only and no more, he might soon have tired of peace and have been found discovering occasions for fresh wars. As it was, he found in himself the power to organize and govern and, in the full exercise of that power, found peace itself alive and interesting enough. Something undoubtedly was lost in the submission of so many to a single will. There was something relaxing in a peace that was far too negatively conceived. But the world had taken so much hurt from a series of wars that peace at any price had become almost a necessity. To this it may be added that the ancients, while accepting war as a part of the natural order and hardly dreaming of abolishing it, saw it for the painful and wasteful thing that it is. "As for war and all its distresses, why should I pick out every painful detail and enlarge on it to you who know?"—so says the Syracusan Hermocrates in Thucydides' *History of the Peloponnesian War*. It is not easy to find examples of the strange sentiment with which some emotional moderns will try to invest it. When, by the special grace of Heaven, the impossible was for the moment realized, and the discordant wills of nations were blended into a harmony, there were few to regret it. It was a general, not a private soldier or a civilian, who lamented, under Claudius, that the good old days of the Republic, with wars always waging, were no more.

The "immense majesty of the Roman peace" impressed the imagination of the world. It was based on two main foundations. The first of these was the emergence of a single power, Rome, strong enough to concentrate military force in her own hands and to enforce her system of government on the world. Her Empire was almost conterminous with ancient civilization, if we omit the distant India and China. All the civilized peoples of the Mediterranean within the natural boundaries of ocean, Rhine and Danube, African desert, Tigris and Euphrates, owned the Roman sway. Beyond the frontiers lived barbarian peoples, still in the twilight of history, incapable of competing for long with their more highly trained neighbors. There was only one exception, Rome's neighbor on the east, the Empire of Parthia, once part of the Seleucid Empire and since the close of the third century B.C. independent. Parthia had a tincture of Greek civilization, but in politics and religion it represented a renascence of the old Iranian ideals. Rome took the limitation as she found it. She did not attempt to push her frontiers further east and accepted Parthia as a power with whom she could negotiate on something like equal terms.

The second foundation of peace was the creation in Rome herself of a stable central government, capable of governing an Empire—a government that has already been sketched in an earlier chapter. Peace and concord here, within the state, were almost more vital than peace abroad, for if they failed disaster must follow. The merits of the system may be measured by the splendid success achieved by the Empire in its first centuries; its defects are revealed by occasional hesitations and partial collapses, until finally they contribute their share to the decline and fall.

If these were the material bases of peace, what were its spiritual bases? First and foremost, the recognition of the destiny of Rome both by the Romans themselves and by their subjects. Second, a complete weariness of the recurrent wars that cost so much and accomplished so little. Third, and third only, a genuine desire for the good life, which required peace for its development. To the ancient moralist the evils of peace were often more apparent than its blessings. He saw that it allowed many indulgences that were necessarily restricted in wartime; he suspected that it relaxed moral fiber. He did not always see that these evils may easily be exaggerated and that even where they exist they very often yield easily to treatment. The supposed degeneration of peace is often due not to any decay of nervous tissue but only to a relaxtion of muscular tension. To the mass of men peace brought freedom from many constraints and distresses. There was a chance of a more moderate level of taxation. The trader found undreamed of possibilities of gain in a world where travel from land to land was becoming easy. Quiet and gentle souls had more chance of living lives of happiness without offence. One would like to be able to add that art, literature, and science enjoyed conditions favorable to their growth, but we shall see later how seriously such a claim must be qualified.

There was a sense of finality and inevitability about the Roman peace. It could be seen as the climax to the history of the Near East, the history of the Greeks and Romans, to which they had long been working up. The generations that followed those first generations, which could remember liberty and carried some unforgotten bitterness with them to the grave, bowed to a destiny manifestly accomplished. As Christianity grew in power, Christian thinkers reflected on the position of the Church in the Roman Empire and concluded that the "world pacified" by Augustus had been under Divine Providence the necessary preparation for the Gospel.

> "No war, or battle's sound
> Was heard the world around; . . .
> And kings sate still with awful eye,
> As if they surely knew their sovran
> Lord was by."

In this new world, what was to be the prevailing attitude towards peace and war? That it would show some change from the past was obvious. Peace had been proved to be possible, under certain conditions and at certain costs. Was it worth them? The answer of the masses was clearly "yes." Almost every single appeal addressed to them under the Empire emphasizes the maintenance or quick recovery of peace as the main object to be attained. But what of the more thoughtful, who could look below the surface and explore beyond the present? Could one accept the Augustan peace as a gain for all time and adapt one's conduct more and more to a life of peace? Or must one admit it to be precarious, buttress it with arms, and do everything possible to keep alive the military spirit with all its hardness as well as with all its strength? The question becomes easier to answer if we divide it up into parts and distinguish the main aspects in which the issue of peace and war under the Empire usually arose.

The only civilized power with which the Empire had to do was, as we have seen, Parthia. With her war came as the occasional interruption to peaceful diplomatic relations. The plain man certainly knew little about the points at issue and cared less—whether Armenia was to be subject to Rome or to Parthia or should be left balanced between the two. Parthia was a distant power, and war with her only seriously affected a part of the Empire, the Eastern provinces and the army. Even if we shift our position and try to see the Parthian problem from the official point of view, it is hard to regard the Parthian wars with any special interest or respect. Rome never made up her mind to conquer Parthia. Parthia never had it in her power to conquer Rome. The wars were fought mainly on questions of prestige and never brought final settlement. When the new Persian Empire ousted the Parthian in the early third century the case was completely changed. The new power was insolent and aggressive and laid claim to the whole of the Eastern provinces. Peace could no longer be bought by minor concessions. The defence of the Tigris and Euphrates became as vital to the Empire as the defence of the Rhine and Danube. Though one cannot offhand call the Sassanid Persians more barbarous than the Parthians, their policy certainly tended to barbarize relations on the whole of the Eastern front.

The main problem for the Empire was the defence of the frontiers against the uncivilized enemies that lay beyond them. Uncivilized elements had at first existed even inside the Empire, but they were very quickly tamed or exterminated. Very little energy needed to be given to maintaining internal peace in the provinces. National revolts were few and tended to decrease in number. The Jews were the only people that pushed their love of independence to the extreme and died as a nation in the act. Over the frontiers lay a new problem. Internal disorders could be corrected or calmed, frontiers could be extended or improved, but you must arrive at last at a point where Roman law ceased to run and the caprice and chaos of the barbarian world began. There has been a tendency in modern times to idealize overmuch the unspoilt virtues of these rough children of nature. Possibilities indeed they had, as afterages have shown. But for the moment they were at a mental age when the love of destruction is overdeveloped, and they needed long discipline and training before their finer powers could find expression. To find value only in these overgrown schoolboys and to see in the ordered life of the Roman Empire only the "chaos" of a world where nationalism was restrained is a sin against the light. The barbarians were surely no pacifists. War to them was a natural activity, restlessness and greed were forces always driving them towards it. The very superiority of the civilization across the frontiers would not always daunt them by its power; it might tempt them with the hope of unlimited loot. Here at last the Empire must make a display of strength—and strength in arms. The frontiers must be carefully surveyed and fortified; legions, supported by auxiliaries, must stand at suitable points; the flexible defences of a long *limes* must be ready to be stiffened and tightened into a great nexus of defence when the occasional trespassers of peacetime were replaced by the insurgent forces of war. Behind this hard fact of military force diplomacy had its play. Kings friendly to Rome could be fostered, jealousy could be sown between neighbors, favorable conditions of trade could be offered, or, alternatively, the barbarians could be pushed back and forced to leave a vacant space near the frontier. In some cases money could be usefully employed. Polite names could be found for subsidies that were really paid to keep restless tribes quiet. The defence of the frontiers was so obviously necessary that, when they were threatened, conscription was still enforced, nor do we hear much objection being raised against it.

The last and least satisfactory of all kinds of war was that produced by an internal breakdown of the imperial government, usually when the succession was disputed after the death or murder of an emperor, less often, when revolt broke out against an emperor in his lifetime and when he lost the constitutional support of the senate. Wars of this class were bound to be wasteful and destructive. They were civil wars and might bring close relatives and friends into conflict with one another. They were in very many cases selfish wars, only really interesting to a limited number of persons on either side —the great majority of whom were ready to obey an emperor in any case and could see little balance of advantage on one side or the other. Two facts will illustrate public opinion on this point. These civil wars were almost always fought to a finish with the elimination of one rival in a comparatively short space of time, and both parties would appeal to the public as the true friends of peace, fighting only to make her more secure. Mars Pacator, to use the language of the coins, was the champion.

With these three distinct classes of war in mind we come back to the question of how the plain Roman regarded peace and war. In general he was certainly for peace; it offered solid satisfactions, while war, with its glittering prizes, was only for the few. He was also more humane (if that is the right word—an ancient moralist might have said more soft) than the upper classes. Wars of the succession were naturally abhorrent to him. It was to be desired that occasion for them should never arise, and if they came, they should be ended as quickly and economically as possible. Occasionally some principle of liberty might seem to be involved. As a rule, it was a fight between two sets of men to gain the responsibilities and prizes of government. Common sense was all in favor of peace at home and against the piling up of armaments, which must increase rather than diminish the danger of military pronunciamentoes. As regards Parthia, the issues at stake would not often be seen clearly or understood in Rome. There would be admission that Roman prestige must be maintained, but no enthusiasm for aggression where aggression seemed never to yield any permanent gain. For the just and necessary wars that had to be fought in defence of the frontiers the support of public opinion was normally forthcoming. Such Romans as disliked military service and war taxes but still valued the advantages of peace and had no alternative policy to war as their defence were pacifists of the wrong kind. Pacifism of this sort was a tendency to be reckoned with, but it could always be made to yield to proved necessity. Only very occasionally, as for instance after the death of Marcus Aurelius when Commodus made a settlement with the barbarians that his best generals considered premature, may the wish to please the public have overriden military policy.

The army actually maintained for the defence of the Roman Empire was extremely moderate in its proportions—under half a million men in all. Conscription, as we have seen, could still be applied in an emergency, but it was seldom necessary to have recourse to it. There were enough ambitious, needy, or desperate citizens, enough willing recruits from the less forward peoples of the Empire to keep the ranks full. The army was essentially professional, and the gap between civilian and soldier yawned wider than ever before. The evil results of this were apparent in the third century, when the armies came much nearer destroying the Empire in civil wars than in maintaining intact the defences of the frontiers. It was a corollary to the limitation of the size of the army that Rome's policy was essentially defensive and not offensive. Augustus had tried once to push forward the frontier from Rhine to Elbe, but the loss of Varus and his legions broke his will to advance. Claudius the First added Britain; Trajan added Dacia to the Empire. But these additions were considered rather as completions of the existing system than as hazardous advances into the unknown. Augustus's deliberate policy still held—to keep the Empire within its boundaries. A forward policy might have offered some attractions. It would have supplied an object of ambition and kept Rome busy assimilating and governing as she conquered. But there were two serious objections—it was a question whether Rome was not already overstrained in the task she had undertaken of civilizing so many backward peoples, and it seemed certain that brilliant conquests must bring forward generals who might be dangerous rivals to the emperor. The emperors themselves were probably more conscious of this second objection.

The only serious form in which pacifism confronted the Roman government was in the Christian Church. The early Christians, whenever it became necessary to define their attitude, were antimilitary in tone. They accepted war as they accepted idolatry, as part of the existing order; they would not accept it, any more than they would accept idolatry, as a desirable employment for a Christian. Christians, of course, served as soldiers—no absolute ban was imposed by the leaders of the Church. But it might easily happen in the course of his profession that a Christian might be involved in idolatrous practices offensive to his conscience, and might, in extreme cases, have to give up either his faith or his calling. The Christian Church, then, was strongly inclined towards the peaceful way of life. It was very conscious of the "bond of peace" between its members. Let others wage wars, if they must! A Christian should have better things to do. Some Christian thinkers even went some way towards formulating a policy alternative to war. They rightly saw the barbarians as the main problem and contended that the right way to deprive them of their power to harm was to civilize and evangelize them rather than break them in war. Thoughtful pagans, here and there, saw a menace to the state in the Christians' attitude towards war. They attacked Christians as unprofitable if not downright disloyal citizens. But the masses of the population were too unwarlike themselves to be easily roused by this line of reproach. It was the actual incidence of such acute evils as famine, plague, or invasion that released the grim cry, "Christiani ad leones."

The pacifism of the early Church was of a rather special character. On one side it was a part of the general protest against the corruptions of the world. On the other it was a natural reflection of political conditions, which themselves suggested peace as the right normal policy. The typical modern objection—that murder is forbidden and that no exception can be made for war—was not so prominent. It is not surprising that the Church, as it grew in influence and numbers, modified its attitude. The great persecution of Diocletian produced its crop of soldier martyrs, but the Church quickly rallied to the banners of Constantine the deliverer. The state was now armed for, and not against, the Church, and few bishops, if any, would dream of forbidding a Christian to bear arms under a Christian emperor. This is not to decide either for or against pacifism as an obligation on Christians—only to state how the problem was seen and judged in one definite historical context.

IX

The Content of Peace:
Science, Art, Literature

ROME, then, if she had not worked the major miracle of eliminating war, had achieved the minor one of subordinating it to peace. If one simply counted the years of complete peace in the Empire and compared them with the years of complete peace in the years that went before it, the difference might not appear so very striking. The Empire had its long, halcyon calm under Hadrian and Antoninus Pius, but it also had the sorry confusions of the civil and foreign wars of the third century. But there was a mighty difference the general testimony of the ancient world proves beyond doubt. Even when there was trouble in some single, outlying province, the great body of the Empire remained at rest, and many provinces could be regarded as so completely pacified that they did not require any standing armies to garrison them.

Rome itself recognized her task—not only to impose peace but also the ways that belong to it, "pacis imponere morem." It was her business to educate the masses of barbarian and backward peoples in the culture she herself had learned from the Greeks. It was a task of enormous difficulty, and, as it is easy enough to show, it was only imperfectly achieved. The subjects of the Empire could not be raised at once in their millions to the level of Pericles and Plato. The barbarians beyond the frontiers had to be left to themselves—a threat of indefinite magnitude for the future: forces already overstrained in assimilation could not be used for expansion. But our debt to Rome for what she did achieve is very great and should be freely acknowledged. Many lovers of Greece cherish bitterness against Rome as the political conquerer of their holy land and refuse to Rome the credit due to her for transmitting the Greek inheritance to the modern world.

It is clear, however, that a peace for which some apologies must be made is not a complete and triumphant success, however justified the apologies themselves may be. Something was lacking in the Roman peace, which cannot be fully explained away by anything that we have yet learned of their religion or their politics. Perhaps, if we try to grasp the content of the Roman peace, we shall come to understand what that defect was. On private life we shall have something to say in the next chapter; for the moment we have to look at a number of activities that lie between public and private life—science, art, literature. They may have concerned a smaller proportion of the population than they do today; but, then as now, they offer a very valuable test of the quality of the civilization in which they grow.

A beginning may be made with serious study, scholarship, and science. Scholarship met with some encouragement from private patrons and even from the state; its fatal defect was that it was far too exclusively concerned with antiquarian research and had no impulse of growth or new life in it. Science in our modern sense hardly existed. Aristotle had suggested and illustrated the methods by which a scientific knowledge of the world might be acquired. But mankind insisted on treating the beginnings of Aristotle as ends and went to sleep on them. Technical competence was high in many branches of engineering and advance had not yet ceased. But there was not that happy combination of theory and practical experiment that is essential for great advances. Mathematics was a special study, often closely associated with philosophy, living in a cloistered seclusion. That it might be used, with enormous effect, to extend man's control of the physical universe would have seemed shocking as well as extravagant. The modern scientist is certain that he holds the keys to many of nature's locked doors; he is sometimes tempted to think that they will unlock the doors of philosophy, too. However uncertain we may be of the philosophical claims of science, however much we may dislike some of the treasures that it is extracting from the store, we accept it as a hope and light of the future. For good or bad, the ancient world was clear of it. Greece hesitated on the threshold, and where Greece hesitated Rome feared to tread. Perhaps it was the exaggerated contempt of the great Greek thinkers for manual labor that kept their theorizing unfruitful and their practical work unenlightened.

Art, intimately related to the ambitions of the emperors and to the service of religion, played a most important part in public life, and, penetrating into private life, added something to the amenities of existence. The Greek was universally admired for his plastic skill and his creativeness. In painting he fell short of later accomplishment, partly through defective knowledge of perspective, partly through poverty of materials. But in sculpture in its varied forms he was supreme. He filled the world with forms of radiant beauty, set in bronze or stone. To this inheritance the Roman in due time succeeded. Victorious Roman generals brought over to Italy no small number of the great Greek originals. Greek artists flocked to the new fount of wealth and patronage and worked for Roman masters. The inspiration came from Greece, and many of the greatest artists continued to be Greeks. But, naturally, gifted pupils of other races, Romans not excluded, learned the art. Rome became the artistic capital of the world. The temples of Rome claimed a good part of the new productions; another fell to the Roman nobility. But it was the emperor who had the widest needs and the deepest purse, and a high proportion of the artistic talent of the world was devoted to the modeling of his statues, the engraving of his coins and medallions, and the narration in stone of such themes as are still to be read on the arches of Trajan and Marcus Aurelius. The trained student of Greek art tends to be impatient of the art of the Empire and to talk very readily of deterioration and decay. He is often more than a little unjust. The traditional skill of the Greeks was far from being exhausted, and the influence of the Roman customer, for whom it now worked, was by no means all for the bad. The Roman lacked the unerring taste of the Greek, but he had a strong positive interest in actual person or fact. Greek art, which, having early learned to model ideal beauty in stone, had continued for centuries to repeat the performance with waning inspiration, stood to gain rather than lose by being forced to undertake tasks beyond the old limited range. There was no general decline of art—only continual modification and adaptation to changing conditions. But a new impulse was needed, and that only came with the Christian Empire and the birth of Byzantine art.

In literature as in art, Rome was a pupil of Greece, but, it is only fair to add, a very apt and ready pupil indeed. The Romans, when they had once mastered the art of self-expression in words and had begun to venture out beyond mere translation, found that they had thoughts of their own to express. They seldom dared to improve on the forms invented by the Greeks; they *did* learn to handle the Greek forms like masters. By the time of Augustus, if not earlier, Roman literature had reached its prime; it could boast of a Cicero, a Catullus, a a Lucretius. For a century and more of the Empire, Latin Literature of the "Silver Age" produced its works of talent, even of genius, its Seneca, its Lucan, its Petronius, its Tacitus. Then the inspiration seems to die away; only at rare intervals does some great figure emerge from a dead background. The creative impulse in literature began to pass from the pagan to the Christian, and it was some time before the latter learned to value form as distinct from content.

The case of history is of special interest because of its intimate connection with political life. It made a special appeal to the practical Roman. By the time of Livy it had passed beyond the stage of mere annals—bare accounts of events in chronological order, with lists of priests, magistrates, and the like—

and had become a powerful weapon of political thought and controversy. Such a tradition could not die out itself in one or two generations, and even tyrannical emperors were shy of direct persecution of an honorable profession. Despite the handicap of living under a "new order," which must not be directly criticized, historians continued, even if at some risk to themselves, to practice their craft. As late as the reign of Trajan a very great historian, Tacitus, could describe the Empire with a mordant and incisive power, which, under a nominal acceptance of the imperial system, suggested the bitterest criticisms of it. After him there is no great name for centuries. The world cannot be altered, why risk persecution by criticizing a system that, whether good or bad, has become inevitable? Let history verge towards her natural end in such an age, imperial biography, beginning with Suetonius and descending to the depths of the worst parts of the *Historia Augusta!* Let the light be focused on the emperor and let the history of the Empire be seen only in relation to him. Let the old serious interest in history as a matter of vital concern to the citizen give way to a mere curiosity as to what the emperor does or suffers. Where so much of ancient writing has been lost, we cannot be quite sure that nothing of serious value has escaped us. On the whole it is safe to say that historical writing declined to a level at which it aimed only at ephemeral fame, and died, as it deserved to die, with the passing taste to which it appealed.

Close to history stands oratory, the branch of literature most congenial to the Roman genius. The Roman knew the value of words in public life and knew how to use them with effect. When Greek elegance was added to Roman seriousness, we get Cicero, a master orator, who may justly challenge comparison with the great Demosthenes. Under the Empire oratory continued to have its uses, in the law courts, even in the senate. But even more than history it drew its life breath from liberty, and with declining liberty it withered away. The complimentary address to the emperor, the panegyric, or the unreal discussion of past dilemmas in the schools of declamation were a sad descent from the grand orations that had swayed the fate of men and nations.

In law the Roman destiny pursued its own course, uninter-rupted—perhaps even assisted—by the Empire. The Romans had a sound natural sense of the need of order in the state and of the sort of legislation in which this order must be expressed. Their first attempts were harsh and narrow; but these defects did not go unobserved, and liberal jurists were soon at work to amend them. As Rome became a power in Italy and then abroad, she enlarged her conception of law to take in a law of nations (jus gentium) by which her own system of law could be checked and amended. The results of this great effort to provide the foundations of social and political life are pre-served for us in the great Codices of Theodosius II and Justin-ian. They are Rome's greatest contribution to the world, and, even by themselves, forbid us to depreciate the work of the Empire that created them.

How did all this affect our plain Roman? Leisure he had in plenty; he had already had it in the later days of the Republic, and the Empire, which finally relieved him of the fierce tasks of war, Lucretius's "fera moenia Martis," gave it in even larger measure. But what did he do with his leisure? He had no radio as we have today. He had not even the public newspa-per; for the "acta diurna," a sort of official chronicle published in Rome, was certainly meager—and official. The published "acta senatus" were probably as little read generally as Han-sard's is today. Books were not exorbitantly dear, and, even with the decline of literature, there was no dearth of inferior wares —scurrilous epigrams, gossiping biographies of the emperors, love stories, and tales of wonder. But reading took up a much smaller part in life than it does with us. The influence of art must not be underrated. Rome clothed herself in such majesty as became an imperial city, and temples, like Vespasian's Temple of Peace, were veritable galleries of art. But, then as now, the capacity of the plain man to appreciate art was strictly limited. The ordinary Roman found life a sort of per-petual holiday, he craved amusement and looked to be amused. The emperors on their side were ready to meet him.

It paid them to keep their many clients in good temper—after filling their bellies, to supply the pleasure of the capital, circus races, gladiatorial shows, and theatrical performances. The passion for the circus ran very near to madness. The different factions—the blue and green, the chief—drew to themselves the partisan zeal that had once fed the political parties. The emperors themselves did not disdain to be known as partisans of one or the other faction. The bloody games of the amphitheatre appealed to even baser instincts than the circus. Decent Romans, if pressed for an excuse, were driven to plead that they encouraged the toughness necessary to a nation that must wage war. But the thirst for blood had sunk deep into the popular heart; the shows lasted through the pagan times and over more than a century of the Christian Empire. Dramatic art in Greece had played an amazing part in public life, as a mirror of the mind and soul of Athens. But imperial Rome had no tragedian like Aeschylus, no comedian like Aristophanes or even Menander. The very art itself was losing its hold and giving place to the novelties of mime and pantomime, which gave full scope to the talent of the actor and dancer, but said good-by to literature and plunged into the depths of dissoluteness and sensationalism. Despite the occasional patronage of an emperor like Nero, the stage had no reputation. For a Roman knight to appear on it was accounted a disgrace, while the profession of actress was closely allied to "the oldest profession in the world." In the western provinces the vices of the capital were industriously copied, as far as means would allow. In the eastern provinces, where the Greek tradition was dominant, there was a healthier tone. There was a widespread enthusiasm for athletic and gymnastic performances and, in general, a distaste for gladiatorial shows. But the general picture of an Empire, wasting its leisure in frivolity—or worse—is unattractive.

The Roman Empire, then, failed to find a full and worthy content for the peace that it had created. The great evils of war and civil strife have often stimulated the creative impulse in literature and art and have brought unexpected compensations for their horrors in their train. There was nothing in the Empire to replace, in any adequate or permanent way, the free energies of the Republic. Security was too much cherished as an end in itself; liberty was so much feared for its dangers that its sweetness was forgotten. The grip of government tightened as resistance slackened. Not that the emperors had any special interest in debasing the amusements of their subjects or in discouraging literature and art; they might even try to appear as their patrons. But there was a fatal defect in the Empire. It could not endure criticism and could not escape criticism, if thought were to continue free. As a beginning of a new world of intelligent peace, the Empire could claim gratitude and acceptance. It is soon found claiming unlimited admiration and obedience as a final end, admitting no discussion or dispute. The Golden Age is restored—but you must not look for any beneficent changes to attest it; you must see the Golden Age in whatever state of things each reign may chance to offer. There was an inflated currency of fine phrases, imperfectly covered by any power or wish to achieve. But, for our own salvation, let us beware of dismissing the men of the Roman Empire as inferior beings, fit only to be flayed by the satirist and then forgotten. There, but for the grace of God, go we!

X

Private Life

So FAR we have been trying to see the Roman world as it must have appeared, not to statesmen, generals, or great thinkers but to the plain man in the street. We have been using him as a measure of the thought of his age—a purpose of which he knew nothing and to which he might have thought himself singularly ill-adapted. Perhaps it is only just to him to leave the larger stage for a moment and make an excursion into private life, to see how he was actually living in the age of which we are making him the representative.

If the evidence of St. Paul and other Christian writers on the sins of the pagan world is taken literally, the picture that emerges of life in the great cities will be a black one. It will be even blacker if we call in the Roman satirists Persius and Juvenal and accept all that they have to say at its face value. But, though such evidence cannot be entirely ruled out of court, it must be checked against other evidence of a less lurid character such as may be found here and there in literature and in the masses of private inscriptions of the Empire. The sensational sins may not vanish, but they will be set in their right place against a background less vicious if more dull.

Sexual morality was notoriously lax, especially in the great cities; "rusticitas," country simplicity, came to be the roué's jibe at virtue. The amusements of the circus and arena certainly fanned the flames of passion. But the collapse of home life and marriage in Rome of the first century was almost confined to the upper classes. With Nero passed much of the old aristocracy, and Vespasian introduced new men and new ways, representative of the sound and hard morality of the Italian farmer. Among the poorer classes the ideals of family affection and loyalty survived. One of the best signs of the times under Trajan was the willingness of the emperor to give and of the people to receive financial help towards rearing families. The chief blot on home life was the exposure of unwanted infants, especially, of course, girls. In times of desperate distress, parents might even sell their children into slavery. Both these ugly sins were rooted in economic strain. There are not wanting some indications that even among pagans a conscience about them was awakening.

Slavery, of course, continued to exist as an institution, though its abuses were largely recognized and its cruelties sometimes mitigated. Christianity made no attempt to abolish slavery at one blow, but it undermined its basis by admitting slaves into the same religious fellowship as their masters. But the supply of slaves was no longer limitless, as it had been in the last few centuries before Christ, and the existing stocks were continually being reduced by emancipation. The trend of the later Empire was not toward slavery, but toward serfdom. The contrast was no longer between a relatively small body of free citizens enthroned and an oppressed mass of slaves below them but between a top-heavy government with hosts of busy and inquisitive officials and whole classes of free citizens shackled to their professions and callings. Those few wealthy citizens who retired to their estates deep in the country and snapped their fingers at authority were really no better than deserters, however bitter may have been the provocation to which they yielded.

Business morality invites criticism in every age. It is usually classed as "low" or "nonexistent." Perhaps in Rome it really was rather low. Fortunes could be made in business and commerce, but there were not the great organized interests of modern times. The man of enterprise worked precariously and uneasily under the eyes of an omnipotent state. There was not the violent and aggressive greed of great trusts and corporations, but there was a great deal of minor trickery and chicanery. For the small man the really corrupting thing was his lack of independence. He would depend in part on some craft or trade, but, in a great city, he was always encouraged to look for a patron. Many a man eked out his living by paying court to some wealthy lord, attending his levees, running his errands, occasionally sitting at his table as a humble guest. But the supreme patron was the emperor himself, with the whole populace as his clientele. "Let me pamper my dear little plebs" were the words of one of the less discreet of emperors. The plain citizen expected to draw his ration of free or cheap corn, to receive every few years his three or four rounds at the largesse, and to be amused and beguiled by a succession of games and shows that gradually came to fill up a large part of the civil year. The mob of Rome—to a lesser degree the mob of all great cities—was a spoiled darling, fed and coaxed to keep it in good temper and to check its proneness to demonstrate against the government. Such a regime did not tend to encourage any great manliness or independence of character.

On social life there was one great and constant check imposed. The government distrusted all private associations as possible focuses of political discontent. It strictly reserved to itself the right to license corporations and to suppress, at will, any that were unlicensed. Though its intention was probably no more than to avoid political danger, its policy was profoundly illiberal. How much of the life of a sound state depends on voluntary associations of men in groups! And how discouraging to men, capable of taking part in such groups, if they may at any time have to face official disapproval!

The decline of the military spirit soon became evident in the cities and caused grave concern to thoughtful observers. The young men from the country, particularly in the fresh and vigorous newer provinces, still flocked to join the ranks. The townsman was sunk in his ease and preferred to have others to do his fighting for him. As an individual, he was subservient to authority and poor-spirited; in mass, at the gatherings of circus or amphitheater, he had a truculence that even emperors of tough fiber dreaded. It is only fair to credit him on the other hand with an occasional gentleness of mood, which surprises us. When under Nero a nobleman had been killed in his house by a slave, and it had been decided to enforce the cruel old law by which all the slaves who had been present in the house at the time of the murder must die, the people of Rome demonstrated vigorously and courageously—though in vain —in favor of the innocent victims. When Galba was murdered in the streets of Rome by the mutinous praetorians, the crowd looked on in a tense silence—the silence, observes Tacitus, that betokens great fear. We might expect this, but also great indignation. When Nero made the Christians the scapegoats for the Great Fire of Rome, many men pitied them for their sufferings, whatever their crimes might have been. No doubt the tender mercies of a crowd are precarious, and there were cases under the Empire of city mobs howling for the blood of the Christians. But the mob of Rome does not stand convicted of such cruelty as its vicious amusements might lead one to expect of it; perhaps its evil instincts were normally glutted by them.

Political interest was at a low ebb. The ordinary Roman no longer voted in the assemblies, and the senate was far beyond his reach. A change of emperor might affect him incidentally for good or evil, but it was really the system that mattered, and the system changed very little whatever particular occupant might be throned in the seat of the Caesars. His demands were not excessive—some degree of peace in the world at large, some measure of stability in the constitution at home— and these the Empire usually met. He certainly expected still to keep his "liberty"; insignificant as he was as an individual, he belonged to a large class, capable of expressing its opinions by public demonstrations and the emperors lived under the terror of this collective disapproval. He was also less likely to challenge attack than the man of rank or wealth. The plain Roman, then, retained his "liberty," in the sense that he was reasonably secure against arbitrary injustice as long as he lived an orderly life and shared in the doles of corn and money and the amusements of the capital that were now the distinguishing privileges of citizens. Political opposition, as it exists in countries where there is an alternative to the ruling government, could not and did not exist. Some questions had been settled by general consent, others by the peace that comes of exhaustion. Political liberty was perhaps a beautiful thing. It looked fine in the old histories, and the philosophers had much to say in its praise. But it had risen to a price at which the world no longer cared to purchase it.

Religion to our plain Roman was a conventional part of the life of the state and was accepted by him as such. If he strayed outside religion, he was more likely to be attracted by astrology or magic than by sceptical philosophy. His religion was very practical—not very lofty or detached, but in its way very real. He was closely fettered to the world of what he saw and handled, but he was no materialist. If he felt his duty towards the gods as a legal rather than an emotional bond, he was in that simply a normal Roman. If he felt the need of something more emotional or personal in his religion, he might find satisfaction in one of the Eastern cults, such as that of the kind and merciful Isis. But even the worship of the Olympian gods allowed more room for personal devotion than is always realized.

There is, it must not be denied, a gulf between our world and that of the ancient Roman. We are at least familiar with the idea of the value of individual life, apart from the social framework in which it is set; of a spiritual world, sensitive to human need; of an afterlife in which we may expect if not gross rewards and punishments at least the solutions to some of the mysteries that perplex us here. In Rome of the early Empire, there was no great tenderness of the individual conscience. Immortality was a vague hope for some, a firm belief for quite a few. To the majority the "Beyond" was either a certain nothingness or a great perhaps.

The chief fault of individual, as of national, life was not so much positive viciousness as nervelessness and lack of tone, an inability to brace oneself to new tasks and new ideas. Our generation can appreciate better than many others how much of this may have been due to overstrains previously endured. What is harder to understand or excuse is the lack of resilience or recuperative power. But our task is rather to understand than to blame and when, as here, we cannot fully understand, honesty requires us to suspend judgment.

XI

Present, Past, and Future

TIME in human experience has three dimensions. Apart from the activities of the present, man has memory to look back to the past and hope to look forward to the future. So far we are all the same. But great differences of attitude towards these three dimensions of time may be observed in different ages and may be found to correspond to vital differences in quality.

The simplest and most natural life is that lived mainly in the present, engrossed in its cares and pleasures. In the nature of things all life must be largely of this character. The animals hardly know any other kind of life, and man, whatever else he may be, is still an animal. But it is possible for man also to live under the ban of the past, ever mindful of its achievements, its examples, its warnings, and fettered by its tradition. This is the extreme conservative attitude, found not only in highly developed states, but also among peoples we are inclined to call primitive. There is a third attitude to be found here and there among individuals but not often sustained for long in a society—the attitude of eager expectation, of stretching out to the future. It will usually involve some neglect of the past and even a certain impatience of the present; its strength lies in its faith that the future has better things to show than have ever been seen yet, in the faith that made "progress" a word to conjure with in the nineteenth century. The three attitudes that we have defined seldom exist pure, but are usually blended more or less with one another. But it is usually possible to specify one or other of them as characteristic of an age or a people.

The Roman combined a great absorption in the present with a vast respect for the past. Its interest in the future was far less intense. Augustus gave the world peace and his successors confirmed and maintained it. Life was secure as it had not been for generations. For the enterprising there were undreamed of opportunities of acquiring wealth; even the feeble and indolent could look for easy subsistence on the charity level in the great cities. Men could choose their walk in life as never before. The demands of the army on the ordinary citizen were relaxed. Volunteers enough could be found in ordinary times to fill the ranks, and conscription was only used in rare cases of emergency. Man had a new freedom to travel the length and breadth of the Mediterranean world. The world seemed to be enjoying a perpetual holiday. The cities of the Empire, restrained from their old feuds, devoted their energies to rivalry in building temples of the emperors and in athletic and musical contests. Everywhere you met the delightful *laetitiae* of life—the races, the games, the public holidays. There was at any rate relative plenty, as the products of earth could pass freely from province to province. There were the baths—an amenity of life fast degenerating into a vice—the feast, the sacrifice, the head crowned with flowers. There was, of course, an ugly side to the picture. The early Christians saw the pagan world with its pomp and pride, its "let us eat, drink, and be merry," passing rapidly away. Even the pagan moralist detected the swarm of hidden vices clustering under the fair surface and affixed his brand of censure. But to judge temperately and candidly we must admit that there was a better natural basis for the good life than there had ever been before and that thousands of men made reasonable and temperate use of their advantages. The "new order" offered to those who would accept it not *otium* (peace) merely but *otium cum dignitate* (peace with honor). A devout Roman might reflect with deep satisfaction that Rome's care for religion had brought her not only material advantage, such as conquest, but also a prosperity that blessed her wherever she went. In course of time deterioration set in. Grave economic defects suddenly revealed themselves in sensational collapses. There was a fatal waste of substance in the ill-conducted and purposeless wars of the third century. But right up to the end a sufficient standard of living was aimed at, if not always achieved, to justify the claim that the Empire meant the restoration of a bliss once enjoyed when the world was young, in a Golden Age before history began.

With this conception our attention shifts naturally from the present to the past. The Roman Empire had in fact an interest in the past that is hard to parallel in any civilization of our Western world. Even in its enjoyment of the present it needed to turn its eyes backward to appreciate what it was enjoying. The ancient myth of the Golden Age in Latium, when Saturn, fleeing from Jupiter, found safe hiding there—an age when there was no want, no strife, when Astraea (Justice), the virgin, still walked with men, not yet driven by their wickedness to take her flight to heaven. Or again, one might think of the babyhood of Jupiter, reared in Crete by the goat Amalthaea whose magic horn, cornucopia, showered plenty of every kind, or of the similar magic horn of the river-god, Achelous, which Hercules broke off in wrestling with him. Hesiod too sets the Golden Age as the first and best of his successive ages of man. It was to this old dream and hope that the world now turned. Virgil hailed Augustus as the promised hero, destined to restore the Golden Age "in fields once ruled by Saturn," and later poets resumed and varied the theme, until it passed into a commonplace of flattery. Each succeeding emperor claims to restore the "Felicitas Temporum" or "Saeculi" ("Bliss of the Times" or "Age"), and the world, ever anxious to be deceived, is cheated again and again by false hopes. There might be a bitter clash between dream and reality. "The times we have to pass are iron, not gold" was the groan of a Christian writer of the third century. But what interests us here is not so much the degree of truth in the claim, as the claim itself. The present is not contemplated in and by itself, it is not interpreted as a stage in fruitful progress; the past is invoked to give it meaning. Once the world was young, innocent, happy. It has grown old in suffering and sin. Even the miraculous powers inherent in the Empire cannot do more than repair the wreck of time and bring back the Golden Age.

But it was not only in this mythical conception that the Roman Empire looked backward. It was deliberatly and obstinately conservative in every part of life. Mankind, after centuries of exciting but wasteful experiment, quite suddenly became aware that the values of life were being squandered faster than they could be replaced. Man took alarm and set to remedy the evil by cutting his losses, by conserving whatever could be conserved, by risking as little as possible on new experiments. A bolder course might promise fuller solutions of the problems, but the world is too timid and dispirited to risk them. The establishment of the Empire can be traced step by step and explained by a sequence of military and political causes, above all by the practical genius and good fortune of the Romans. At the center there was need of innovation, of revolution even; only in a very limited sense was it true that the Empire was the continuation of the free Republic, the emperor the successor of the republican magistrate. But it was the urgent need of the world for peace as much as the military triumphs of the Roman generals that made the Empire possible; it was the same need that directed it in the course it must take. The Empire was created out of revolution to end revolution in detail, to give the civilized peoples stability and order, to establish frontiers that could be firmly held, above all, to check the drain of power and give the world space to convalesce. The historian Livy, whose work is no less closely related to the work of Augustus than the poems of Virgil and Horace, records the models (exempla) of the great men of early Rome as encouragements and warnings to later generations. It soon appeared that the Empire no longer gave scope to the exercise of the old Republican virtues and that it demanded new qualities of its own. But the Republican ideal lingered on as in a dream long after it had ceased to have such place in waking life. We can perhaps best compute its worth by a negative test, by the failure of the Empire to develop anything to replace it. Praise of the ideal basileus and his kingdom did indeed flourish but more on the Greek than on the Roman side of the Empire; and, as we are learning over again by bitter experience, it is a sad mistake to pretend that the real life and worth of a state rests on the merits of one or a few.

As in political thought the conservative tendency prevailed, so in art and literature. The great creations of Greek artists from Phidias and the Parthenon onwards were inimitable, unrivaled—*ktemata eis aei*—possessions for eternity but not spurs to new achievement. So too with the writers and the poets. Greece had set examples of excellence in every branch of literature that might serve as models for Roman apprentices, but Homer, the tragedians, and Plato could never be superseded. The older Latin authors lacked the beauty and originality of the Greeks, but they had assumed the dignity of age; if you could not admire them for their excellence, you could at least study them for their antiquarian interest. There was a good deal of harmless if rather futile study of the obsolete, which reached its height under the quiet rule of Antoninus Pius; it was the affair of scholars, relatively few in number, but it did not run counter to the general spirit of the age.

In general the stock of ideas was drawn almost entirely from the past. Discussion of politics and warfare will go back to Herodotus and Marathon, if not to Homer and Troy. The great examples of early Roman history—Tarquin the Proud, Brutus, the first consul, brave Horatius—will still serve as warnings or encouragements to later times. That the schools of rhetoric should draw their themes from the past, should debate with Hannibal whether to advance on Rome after Cannae, was not surprising; dead themes were safer than living ones. But the tendency to hang onto the past went beyond the schools of rhetoric and through the whole Empire. The treasures of old experience were being continually borrowed, but the present did not contribute its fair share of alertness and skill that might have enabled it to repay its debt with interest. The heritage of the past, inexhaustible as it was, gradually forfeited much of its power to stimulate and encourage.

There was something lacking to the Roman both in his enjoyment of the present and in his return to the past. He had a very feeble sense of the remaining dimension of time, the future. "The rapture of the forward view" is very hard to find in any corner of the Roman Empire. Evolution from the savage state to the civilized had been imagined and studied; it had been introduced to Rome by Lucretius in the fifth book of his *De rerum natura*. But continued evolution to higher stages of civilization, though a natural corollary of the advance from the savage to civilization, was not readily accepted. The progress so dear to the nineteenth century, the age of triumphant science, was as yet an unknown god. Men were tired of the burdens of active life, tired even of the burden of thinking out its problems. So much had already been accomplished, and what more could be done? The Roman looked forward to an indefinitely long continuation of the imperial rule of Rome. The subjects of the Empire came more and more to acquiesce in the Roman hope. The Christian Church had its own dream of the future, but it was not of this world; under providence it was the rule of Rome that warded off the coming of antichrist and the terrors of the last times.

The motto of the state then might be taken to be "as things have been they remain"; *cras fore melius,* "tomorrow will be better than today," was applied, if at all, only to private life. The slogans that represent the general attitude to the future are not "progress" or "reform," but *aeternitas, perpetuitas, felicium temporum reparatio,* "eternity, perpetuity, restoration of the times of happiness"; these were old themes, introducing many a fine passage, but never a new note. The eternity of Rome, the eternity of the emperor—these twin themes between them almost exhaust the Roman attitude to the future. Rome has received Empire from the gods as hers in permanent possession; she is in the political order what sun and moon are in the natural. The emperor shares in the Roman destiny. He has a larger share in the divine nature than the ordinary man, he stands nearer than him to eternity, the divine world. He may be thought of as lent to earth by the gods for a season, until in due course he returns to his native heaven.

The life of the Empire then, deep-rooted in the past, was concentrated on present interests; towards the future it was apathetic. Politics had fossilized into a mighty, inelastic system. Art and literature, except when caught up into the service of the new order, lacked originality and aim. Science was not yet born. The result was a vague distress and lack of tone, a hopelessness that betrayed a flagging vitality. Once and again an individual genius, like the Emperor Hadrian, could break the spell and dream his own dreams of the future. But there were few like him, and the spirit of the age was against them. Yet life, even if it seems to stagnate, never really stands still. In the aging body of the Empire a new spirit was at work—a spirit destined, when that body lay dead, to find new forms in which it could live on.

XII

Transitus

THE METHOD that we have followed up to now has involved a certain error, foreseen, but deliberately risked. Experiences actually spread over several centuries have been brought together to form more effective general pictures. It is to be hoped that the gain of this method outweighs the loss. But it will be well in this final chapter to do something to restore the balance, by stressing instead of neglecting the process of development, and by making the transit from old to new within the Roman Empire the main object of our study. We shall first have to see in what the change consisted and to follow it up in politics, religion, war, and society. We must then observe how the mind of the ordinary Roman reacted to these changes—in particular how his religious beliefs took a new direction. Finally it will be of interest to look back on the process from its end, the growing barbarian menace and the triumph of Christianity.

Under the sway of eternal Rome evolution seemed to have reached a halt. Peace and order, if not guaranteed in perpetuity, were securer than ever before. A long climb up dangerous crags had led out on to a ledge where one could rest. The heats and follies of adolescence had been outlived. The world had reached a sensible midage, soon to verge towards decline. It was time to enjoy the acquisitions of the past and no more to gamble on uncertain futures. But rest like motion may be apparent as well as real, and under the surface of an Empire apparently stagnant change was ever preparing. The issues were slow to appear in action—it was not until the third century that they began to break through with explosive force—but they were growing in secret very much earlier. To the Roman conservative, change, if it could not be quite ignored, would appear simply as an evil, a loss of values to be deplored, a decline from old discipline and good morals. But the conservative, triumphantly secure as he may be when allowed to shelter under his own premises, is helpless outside them. The Roman Empire was to prove in the end no more than a rather specially successful caravansary among the many in which traveling mankind has bivouacked.

Regarded as a political system, the Roman Empire might seem to be the absolute end of a process. The city-state of Rome, driven by fate and circumstance to break its natural bounds and form the center of an Empire, had forced its constitution into correspondence with its fortune. It had created the convenient fiction of the "first citizen" of a free Republic, who was yet in fact more powerful than any potentate, who became the model of all emperors to follow. What further change was possible here? The sequel showed. The constitutional pretence that veiled despotism gradually thinned and fell away. The Empire came to be recognized as a plain autocracy and, in forms as well as in fact, approximated to the one other great lordship on earth, the renascent Persian Empire, which replaced the Parthian in the third century. So far there is nothing to surprise us—nothing but a shedding of pretence and a substitution of fact for fiction. But the change went deep, and it was only seen on the surface when it had been accomplished below. The political lawyer could write of the "first citizen" of a Republic, entrusted by the will of the citizens with powers that were virtually absolute, and could show how such an institution of necessity became permanent so that a line of "first citizens" followed one another in succession. But while no one was concerned to contradict the theory, there was in fact a rapid decline towards a much simpler and lower idea. In the Greek half of the Empire the emperor was simply the king;

the Roman avoided the word but accepted the fact. To the ordinary man the emperor became more and more the Great King, the King of Kings; he could be clearly seen under his disguise.

What other developments are theoretically possible in a state that cherishes the ideal of liberty but is compelled to arm its government with exceptional powers it is hard to say; we lack experience to guide us. But there was one development gradually realized in Rome that grew directly out of the extent and complexity of the Empire. However vast the labors that a conscientious emperor might undertake, there were limits to human capacity. To carry out his will he must depend on a great and highly organized service, both military and civil. It was this that gave the later Empire its special character—half an autocracy, half an autocratic bureaucracy, dependent of course on the emperor but able to defend its own interests and maintain its own powers because it was the emperor's essential form of expression. Why no successor to the emperor ever arose out of some overgrown branch of the service is hard to say. In the third century there seemed for a time to be a possibility that the praetorian prefect, the commander of the imperial guard, might usurp the real power, governing for the emperor as a *roi faineant*. There was evidently some balance of power that checked the rise of the prefect, but if he had broken through, there was nothing to prevent him from dethroning the emperor and taking his place.

To some extent the changed position of the emperor depended less on the emergence of new facts than on the recognition of old ones. But in two points at least vital changes were taking place. The senate, the traditional and honored representative of the Roman people, gradually lost its authority and ceased to take even that limited share in government that Augustus had reserved to it. Down into the third century it still held some influence as the body that conferred legitimacy on the emperor, but in general its powers were lapsing, while the knights, the second order of the Roman aristocracy, filled the vacant place. The senators, afraid of political dangers and allured by the attractions of ease, surrendered to "military men of no education the power of tyrannizing over themselves and their children." For the army, with knights in the chief commands, was coming into a new prominence. It swore allegiance to the emperor and maintained him in power; it could make and unmake him. Once this was fully recognized, the normal way into office was by military pronunciamento, the normal way out by assassination. Diocletian by various judicious measures brought the army back under control. He reduced the size of the legion, strengthened the central army at the expense of the armies of the frontiers, and removed the person of the emperor to a safe distance from his loyal *commilitones*. But even after Diocletian the emperor, for his own safety, had to treat the soldiers with all possible consideration. In the fifth century the old evil recurred under a new form. The new commanders-in-chief, the *magistri militum,* supported by bodyguards devoted to them personally, kept the lawful emperors in a condition of virtual bondage.

So much for the central government and the army. What of Rome and the provinces? The origin had been perfectly clear. Rome was mistress of the world; Italy was her close ally and shared in her privilege. The rest of the world was subject; but subjection was mitigated by the gradual admission of individuals and communities to a share in Roman citizenship. In one sense the end was reached when Caracalla in A.D. 212 extended citizenship over the whole Empire. Another end was more slowly and gradually reached during the third century. Rome and Italy began to lose their special privileges. Provincial cities became centers of administration and came to rival Rome. By the age of Diocletian the Empire was essentially one in privilege over its whole extent. But it was a leveling down, not up. The provinces were not promoted to the level of Rome and Italy; Rome and Italy fell to theirs.

Throughout the Empire a process was at work by which the more backward districts gradually advanced towards the higher levels of civilization. It found its chief expression in the growth of city life. This process was particularly successful in the great district of Illyricum and, so long as the Empire had any real vitality, was never completely suspended. The Empire was essentially a confederation of city-states; the cities were the cells out of a conglomeration of which the Empire was built up. It was through defect at this vital point that the Empire finally fell. The cities, cut off from active political life, entered on extravagant programs of building and became deeply involved in debt. The Imperial Government found itself compelled to intervene and take a share in the responsibility by appointing officers to control the finances. Local independence thus sustained yet another blow. Then, as the financial position deteriorated, the task of raising the taxes became steadily harder. The government shifted the burden on to the shoulders of the local senators (*curiales*) and membership in these local senates, which had once been treasured as a high honor, became a deadly liability from which men tried at any risk to escape. This decay of the municipalities was either a cause or a significant symptom of the waning strength of the Empire. The city began to lose that supremacy it had so long held over the country districts that served its needs and lived under its ban. The rich and powerful began to withdraw from the cities to their country estates, where they might defy the tax collector, harbor refugees from justice, and in general comport themselves as little lords. The central government was beginning to lose its grip, and something like the elements of a feudal system began to appear.

Economics as we all know is a difficult subject to study, even where the material is plentiful. Where our data are as imperfect as they are for the Roman Empire, it is imposible to trace causes and effects with any certainty. All that is possible is to indicate some main tendencies. The Empire certainly brought at first a considerable rise in prosperity, owing to peace and settled conditions and an ordered coinage. There was no free trade within the Empire, which was divided into a number of great customs districts; but the mere freedom of travel that peace insured must have had a most stimulating

effect on trade. With the East the balance of trade was un-
favorable to the Empire, which imported spices and similiar
luxuries and, lacking exports to balance the account, paid in
gold and silver that ought not to have been spared. With the
barbarians, north, south, and west, the case was better. The
loss of bullion was at worst not serious, and some markets
were opened up to imperial manufactures. There was no serious development of private capitalism. Great fortunes were
made in business, especially by freedmen. But unless their
owners fell into disfavor with the emperor and lost their goods
by confiscation, their heirs within a few generations would be
found to be senators, with their fortunes invested in land. The
state itself was the one great capitalist and, except to a limited
extent in the fourth century, it did not direct its immense resources towards commercial enterprise. Wholesale production
in private hands did not develop very far. Certain articles,
such as fine pottery from Gaul, might be produced in mass for
export, but there was nothing to correspond to the great financial corporations of modern Europe and America. The opportunities offered by the imperial peace to enterprise and
investment were either neglected or very carefully checked.
The coinage was soundly planned and firmly controlled, and
for a long time it commanded complete confidence. It rested
at first on a basis of gold and silver, later on gold alone;
bronze and copper were used all along as token money under
senatorial control. But the emperors after a time began to avail
themselves of the dangerous expedient of inflation. They
issued denarii in increasingly debased metal without adequate
gold cover. For a time public confidence held and all looked
well. But the final result was what one might have antici-
pated. Quite suddenly confidence gave way and found nothing to sustain it. Complete financial chaos ensued, and recovery was slow and precarious. For a time in the late third
century the state itself half abandoned a money system, both
receiving and paying dues in kind. In the fourth century, after
the reforms of Diocletian and Constantine, money seems to
have resumed its proper function. There was now a plentiful

and regular coinage in gold, with silver gradually coming back into its place beside it and a subsidiary coinage in a kind of silvered bronze. The gold unit, the solidus, however, is not tariffed at any fixed number of bronze units; it is bought and sold in the market at shifting rates. Even today we are not well informed about the more intricate points of political economy. The Romans knew far less. By abuse of inflation the emperors had come near to shipwrecking the state in the middle of the third century. The lesson was not entirely lost on them. There was henceforward a lively sense of danger, and the gold coinage at least was kept steady. But the emperors were too ready to fall into the impatience characteristic of ill-informed autocracy. Faced with such unwelcome symptoms as the great rise of prices in the years just before A.D. 300 and unable to diagnose their cause, they proceeded to issue edicts, laying the whole blame on the wickedness of evil-minded citizens and threatening such and such violent punishments if the evils did not at once abate. This method of treating disorders of the economic system as private crimes and punishing them as such had no more success than it deserved.

The Empire of Diocletian and his successors was a sadly harassed body, haunted by fears. It looked back and saw how narrowly it had escaped destruction in the ruins of the third century; it remembered the slow and painful steps by which it had climbed to recovery. It had been compelled to submit to reorganization at almost every point in order to survive. It had no exuberance of energy, no confidence in its power to meet sudden emergency. It began to calculate nicely just how much would be wanted for every need and just where it was to be found. That way fossilization lies. If you take a survey of the state, decide how many men must be kept under arms, how many in the civil service, how many in essential state services, how many on the land, and how much money must be raised in taxes, and if you found at the last only a precarious balance, you begin to fear that any free movements, such as individuals left to themselves tend to take, will upset the whole machine. The next step follows as a logical necessity. You do your best to eliminate all individual wish and choice and prescribe everything in advance by general ordinance. The soldier shall continue to be a soldier, the civil servant to be a civil servant, the shipper of corn the same, and their sons and grandsons after them. The property that has paid tax under one owner shall remain subject to the same tax, however it passes by purchase or inheritance. Left to itself the state might break into fragments; bound in chains of ordinance, it may still survive. How long? One special example of the virtual enslavement of the individual comes into great prominence in later history— the medieval serf, free in person but tied to the soil, *glebae adscriptus*. In the state system of Diocletian he was only one of a number of serfs, each bound to his own sod. A slave state indeed! And even the Jovian emperor himself was not so very free. Slavery as an institution was on the decline, but there was little advantage if it was merely replaced by serfdom. Men were escaping the bondage of individual masters only to fall under that of economic necessities, which they could neither comprehend nor control.

Abroad it was only superficially that the position seemed little changed. In the East the aggressive Persia had replaced the easier Parthia. But after the fury of the first onslaughts, when it threatened to overwhelm Syria and Asia Minor, it was rather a constant vexation than a serious menace to life. But on the other frontiers, the danger grew from year to year. The barbarians, the nations outside civilization, stirred in a new restlessness. They had learned to know more and more of the wealth accumulated within the Empire; they had occasionally ventured to steal and taste; they began to despise the man of peace as much as they coveted his goods. The barbarians assimilated Roman methods of warfare, while no epoch-making new inventions were forthcoming to set off their rude vigor. The time was past when Rome could debate whether to hold the barbarians at arm's length or to admit them slowly and discreetly and use them as its friends. The question now was whether the frontiers could be held at all, and it was answered more and more in the negative. After many a stubborn fight, many a cunning delay, many an enlistment of the foe in the Empire's defence, the floodgates broke at last and the Western Empire sank under the barbarian tide. The East passed, by what still seems a miracle, without disaster through perils hardly less extreme. Byzantium preserved under the Roman name a culture and religion beside which the Frank for centuries looked little better than a savage.

Such were the external changes forced by time on a civilization that resisted change as an enemy to its inmost being. What accompanying changes can be traced in thought? Some there were that were absolutely demanded by the external changes we have been discussing. The man in the street was compelled to adjust himself to the new order—an emperor who was no longer in any sense a republician magistrate but an irresponsible autocrat, a supreme state with an inflated civil service, a society in which initiative and free movement were almost lost. He turned to those interests that can escape the stifling pressure of the state—his private life, his pleasures, and his religion. He probably did not find the adjustment so very hard; he had felt in his bones how things were going sooner than the constitutional lawyers.

With the changed position of Rome and Italy our plain Roman could no longer enjoy all his old pride of race. Prestige Rome still enjoyed, but it was more like the prestige of Athens than of the Rome of Augustus—a prestige based on sentiment and interest in the past. All subjects of the Empire were now Romans and, in their new Roman pride, held themselves haughtily aloof from the mere barbarian. It may even be doubted how much pure Roman quality our Roman himself possessed. After so much immigration from abroad, so much emancipation of slaves, what actual distinction was left him beyond the mere fact of domicile in Rome? Some scholars actually attribute the spread of Eastern religions in the West to the influx of foreign blood. There is not sufficient evidence surviving to answer the question with authority, and in any case our answer will be influenced by our views on race. We can at any rate reject with complete conviction the extreme absurdities of modern race theory. Physical race is only one of several factors, not always the most important, that combine to form a nationality or culture.

The deterioration of economic conditions and the increasing pressure of taxation and exaction had simply to be endured —no amount of arguing or talking could alter that. That was one of the main causes of the decline of the West. The Roman citizens, *fessi oneribus,* "exhausted by their burdens," had no longer the will to resist that barbarian pressure that seldom relaxed—and that could not be much worse than the tax collector. Why the East survived while the West fell is a mystery not yet completely solved. Perhaps the answer lies simply in the superiority of Constantinople as a strategic position to Rome. But what would have happened if some accident had occurred at the critical moment to divert the eyes of Alaric towards Constantinople rather than the West?

The development of religious thought followed its own internal course, only partially determined by the changed political configuration. The principate itself and, even more, the absolute monarchy must have tended to the advance of monotheism, or at the least to the worship of one supreme god above the many. The new perils in the world abroad, the realization of the precariousness of Rome's position, made men ask anxiously what sins of theirs had merited the divine displeasure. The old pagan could only say that the gods were angry because their worship was neglected. The new Christian answer was far more convincing. Suffering and disaster were no new things; the particular form they were taking was determined by Divine Providence, not without relation to the shortcomings of the Roman Empire.

The religion of the state remains of vital importance throughout. It was here that paganism fought its last great battle against Christianity. The old gods, brought into harmony under the supremacy of Jupiter or Sol Invictus, are grouped as companions and preservers round the person of the emperors. They themselves are the vehicles of heavenly powers and virtues, and they are treading the path of service to the euhemerist heaven. The sense of the dependence of Rome on the heavenly powers grew rather than waned with the increasing menace to her position. But the world was tired of the confusions and absurdities of pagan philosophy, tired too of the inadequacy of pagan practice. When Constantine decided that the true "virtue" lay with the God of the Christians, it was not slow to accept his decision.

What changes in thought did the Christian revolution involve? It satisfied reason by discarding masses of illogical legend and practice and setting before men the worship of the One, True God. It satisfied the heart by making Him essentially good and by relating Him to man in His Son, Jesus Christ the Lord. It taught clearly and without reserve that the offering of a pure and humble heart is the true sacrifice. It insisted on the duty of kindness to the sick and the prisoner. It accepted the Roman Empire and the Roman emperor, its head, as parts of the divine order. It could not countenance the worship of the emperor as god, but it could steadfastly pray for his salvation and could accept his rule as "by the grace of God." The pagan grumbled that the Roman virtus was lost, that a new religion of softness and insincerity had ousted the old sanctities. However true it may be that a tender Christian conscience might be embarrassed by the hard necessities of politics, it was not by any lack of moral toughness that the Christian Empire fell. The independence of Western Christianity from the state did not precede, it followed the fall.

It was in A.D. 311 that Galerius on his death bed issued his edict of toleration, which was soon to be taken up by Constantine and Licinius in the famous Edict of Milan. It was in A.D. 324 that Constantine swept away Licinius, who was relapsing to paganism, and confirmed the position of Christianity as the favored religion. But it was not till the reign of Theodosius the Great (A.D. 378–395) that paganism was proscribed, not till Justinian in the sixth century that it was finally driven out of the schools of philosophy in Greece. There was a strange lull at the turn of the tide. Christianity was dominant and enjoyed imperial favor, but the general principle was toleration;

let each man worship God as he thinks best. So far as there was persecution, it was more in the Church than outside; Athanasian and Arian fought one another with a savagery that stirred the bitter amusement of the pagan. Something vital was at stake. The Athanasian stood for Christianity as a special revelation; the Arians, however saintly and scholarly many of their leaders were, were really introducing a new paganism under Christian forms. The spirit in which the battle was fought seems to have been uniformly pagan on both sides. Julian the Apostate made one last attempt to turn the tide and substitute for Christianity a new paganism that should copy much of the best of Christian practice. But there was no real life in his system, and it died with him. Meanwhile the imperial government continued to address to our plain Roman—we may think of him now as the ordinary citizen in all parts of the Empire—its warnings and encouragements. Its language is cautious and compromising. It still glorifies the person of the emperor as "restorer of the state" or as "vanquisher of the barbarian peoples," but it does not deify him. It still holds out the promise of victory, peace, security, salvation, but no longer appeals to the gods of Olympus. At the same time it omits, apart from a few rare instances, any definite reference to Christianity except as subordinate parts of a type, as mint marks. It is the same convention that one meets in the literature of the fourth century, where vague references to the "divine power" can be interpreted by the reader to suit his own belief.

It was not till a little before A.D. 500—a date outside the period of our present inquiry—that the transit was complete, that the Roman Empire had finally parted in two, that the West went down before the Ostrogoths, Franks and Vandals, while the East entered on its long watch as sentinel of civilization on the Bosphorus. But almost a century earlier a great Christian writer, Saint Augustine, in his *City of God,* had foreseen what was to come. The Church had always claimed that it had a destiny of its own, independent of any political system. But after the first expectation of a speedy end of the age had vanished, it had fully accepted Rome as a part of the Divine Providence and had prayed for the maintenance of the Roman Empire, which alone, under God, kept off the terrors of the last times. When a danger long threatened became fact, when Alaric sacked Rome and darkness drew in on the West, the Christian had to face a new future. Rome the Eternal was after all to fall; must the Church fall with her? It was then that Saint Augustine, in a splendid flight of prophetic imagination, rose above the dark present and saw the task assigned to the Church of carrying over the great heritage into the future. Man was no longer to have one home—his earthly state—but a second—the "City of God"—into which he was admitted at baptism. The way was open for the dualism of the Middle Age, with its great balance of power between emperor and pope. The end is not yet, for ever since the revival of the state in modern times the Church has been trying, without any final success, to define its attitude towards it.

The Christian revolution is probably the most fateful transit ever yet achieved by man. If we fix our eyes on its essential features—its clarification of thought, its deepening and purifying of moral life, its splendid democracy—we cannot fall into the error of belittling what it has done for us. But paganism is apparently something permanent in human life, a substratum not fully eliminated, and it is entrenched behind a vigorous common sense of its own. In much of what must be classed as Christian history there is very little sign of any attempt to express the new faith—only the re-emergence, under Christian names, of strivings as old as sin.

History reveals two great movements, always interlocked yet essentially independent of one another—the movements of states and of peoples, in which the individual plays a humble and subordinate part; and the development of the individual soul, which, strong in its own freedom, need care little for political rise and fall, for *res Romanas perituraque regna,* "the might of Rome and kingdoms doomed to die." Hitherto it is in the first of these movements that the strength of paganism has been seen, the strength of Christianity in the second.

Whether the quickening power of Christianity is ever to work in the life of groups and societies, as it has worked in the life of individuals, may be doubted. Perhaps it is always to be a leaven, slowly leavening the lump of societies that, collectively regarded, are still pagan. Perhaps the attempt to evangelize the state in any deep sense must fail; but one is sometimes inclined to doubt whether the attempt has ever yet seriously been made.